Raising the Dead

Sermons of Howard G. Hageman

D1521171

Gregg A. Mast, Editor

© 2000 Wm. B. Eerdmans Publishing Co.
255 Jefferson Ave. S.E., Grand Rapids, MI 49503
All rights reserved

Printed in the United States of America

04 03 02 01 00   5 4 3 2 1

ISBN 0-8028-4884-2

The Historical Series of the Reformed Church in America

No. 34

Raising the Dead

Sermons of Howard G. Hageman

including the republication of
We Call This Friday Good

Gregg A. Mast, Editor

Wm. B. Eerdmans Publishing Co.
Grand Rapids, Michigan

The Historical Series of the Reformed Church in America

This series has been inaugurated by the General Synod of the Reformed Church in America, acting through its Commission on History, for the purpose of encouraging historical research and providing a medium wherein this knowledge may be shared with the academic community and with the members of the denomination in order that a knowledge of the past may contribute to right action in the present.

General Editor

The Reverend Donald J. Bruggink, Ph.D.
Western Theological Seminary

Commission on History

Gerald F. De Jong, Ph.D., Orange City, Iowa
Sophie Mathonnet-Vander Well, M.Div., Pella, Iowa
Christopher Moore, New York, New York
Jennifer Reece, M.Div., Princeton, New Jersey
Jeffrey Tyler, Ph.D., Hope College, Holland, Michigan

Dedicated to

the parish and congregation

of the

North Reformed Church

Newark, New Jersey

Notes on the Text

In many ways the heart of this book is found in parts 1 and 2, which include a reprinting of Howard Hageman's book, *We Call This Friday Good*. Since its first and only printing in 1961, friends and students of Howard have hoarded their own copies or sought for one to share with colleagues. This poetic and profound sermonic series on the last seven words from the cross was preached by Howard at the North Reformed Church in Newark, New Jersey, where he served as pastor for twenty-eight years. Because *We Call This Friday Good* was dedicated to the parish and congregation of the North Reformed Church, we have chosen to offer this volume with the same dedication. During the cataloging of the almost two thousand sermons Howard left us, we discovered a series preached on the same words, to the same congregation, during Holy Week of 1968, immediately following the assassination of Dr. Martin Luther King, Jr. As one would expect, these two sets of sermons, so very timeless and timely, provide a remarkable opportunity for us to continue to learn from a preacher who committed his life and vocation to the Word.

The balance of the volume focuses our attention on four festival days of the Christian year. Howard would have been the first to confess that these sermons are probably not among his best. At the same time, having tried for almost a quarter of a century to bring new life to old stories, I am convinced that many preachers would welcome these beautiful and provocative gifts from a master homilitician. Almost all of the sermons were preached at North Reformed Church, a downtown, tall steeple church in the heart of an old eastern industrial city. The sermons preached in the 1940s and 1950s allude to an era in which there was a growing fear of the danger unleashed by the atomic age. The sermons preached in the 1960s and 1970s are particularly conscious of the church's deep and abiding commitment to racial justice and ecumenical understanding.

The title for this volume has been taken from one of Howard's favorite admonitions to Sunday morning preachers: "You have twenty minutes to raise the dead." I hope that you will sense the joy that Howard brought to this awesome responsibility.

A Tribute to Howard G. Hageman

This volume is published with the assistance of many friends of Howard G. Hageman. The following individuals and organizations have helped to underwrite the expense of its publication. It is presented with gratitude and affection in memory of Howard, our teacher, colleague, pastor, and friend.

Names appear as provided by the subscribers

The Rev. Sims Akins, Jr.
David Alexander
The Angus Family
Dave Armstrong
John J. & Rhea V. H. Arnold
Charles & Carol Ashley
Charles & Rieneke Ausherman
George W. Barrowclough
Robert W. Barrowclough
Edward Baskerville
Mrs. Catherine Bell
Peter W. Berry
Mrs. Ludwig R. Binder
Blooming Grove Reformed Church
The Rev. Dr. Joseph G. Bodnar
Raymond & Norma Boehm
Jane Z. Bogert
Mary Bon
James H. Booth
Wilbur R. Brandli
The Rev. Richard L. Brihn
Mrs. Jean Brinser

H. "Shorty" Brown
Lynn Brown
Scott & Kay Brown
William C. Brownson
Donald J. Bruggink
Elaine & Elton Bruins
Helen & Merrick Bryce
C. David Buchanan
The Rev. Warren Burgess
The Rev. Neal S. Busker
The Rev. Robert E. Butcher
Ekdal J. Buys
Robert Byrnes
William Cameron
Wilbur D. Canaday
The Rev. Alvin Cason
The Rev. Teresita Chang
The Rev. Dr. William H. Chavis, Jr.
Jack & Deb Cherry
Janet R. Conti
The Rev. Martin L. Cox, Jr.
Carol Cortelyou Cruikshank
Pastor Kenneth Cumberbatch

Albert & Joan Daly
The Rev. Prof. Horton Davies
Fran De Jong
Herman D. De Jong
Robery Delany
The Rev. Harold De Roo
Anna & David Dethmers
John R. De Velder
The Rev. Walter De Velder
John F. De Vries
Roger De Young
Bob & Donna Drum
The Rev. Robert B. Dunbar
The Rev. Stephen J. Eckert
Robert C. Engel
John C. Engelhard
Mark & Pamela Ennis
The Rev. Frank Estocin
Dr. Ramon A. Evangelista
Noreen Fairbank
Shirley Farrell
James D. Folts
Russell & Grace Franck
E. Helen Gardner
Jeff & Moira Gargano
The Rev. & Mrs. Stephen Giordano
The Rev. Doris Glaspy
The Rev. Dr. Robert L. Gram
Donald Hastings
Dr. & Mrs. Andrew Hendricks
Warren J. Henseler
Arnold & Lucretia Hess
Maryellen Hess

I. John Hesselink
Dr. John E. Hiemstra
Jon Hinkamp
Joan & Marvin D. Hoff
The Rev. Bruce J. Hoffman
Edward T. Hoffman
Steven Hoffman
Mary G. Holden
Hope College Department of Religion
Betty & Walter
Nancy & Rick
David
Renee House
Elizabeth Huba
Earle W. Hutchison
Kent E. Huyck
Wilbur & Martha Ivins
Allen Jager
The Rev. Deb Jameson
The Rev. Paul G. Janssen
The Rev. Dr. Lynn & The Rev. Jeff Japinga
The Rev. David W. Jenks
Evelyn L. Johnson
The Rt. Rev. William C. Johnson
Helen Jones
Dr. Leonard V. Kalkwarf
Mary & Norman Kansfield
Mr. & Mrs. Thomas P. Kelly
Thomas A. Kendall
Marjorie W. Kenney
Ruth & Khodamorad Kermani

The Rev. Dr. Martin Kessler
Bob Kirk
The Rev. Jeffrey A. Kisner, Ph.D.
Carl & Helen Kleis
Mark A. Kraai
Louis J. La Fazia
Samuel C. La Penta
Clara T. Lasselle
Craig L. Lawson
Inok Lee
Mark G. Lemmenes
Roger Leonard
Ronald D. Lokhorst
Robert Long
Ronald Lowry
H. E. Luben
Douglas R. Mac Donald
John Magee
Robert T. Marsh
Neal & Stella Mast
Vicki A. Mast
Steve & Sophie Mathonnet-
 VanderWell
Peter G. Maurer
The Rev. Richard O. McEachern
Dr. Daniel J. Meeter
Bruce Menning
The Mercersburg Society
The Rev. John H. Meyer
Al Miller, in memory of Barbara
Richard A. Miller
Audrey R. Ming
The Rev. Lydia N. Miranda
Frederick & Doris Mold

Susan Molloy
E. Andrew Mondore
Edward Mondore
Barbara Morgan
Jane B. Moriarty
Paul R. Moyer
Fred & Barbara Mueller
The Rev. Joe Muyskens
Carol & David Myers
James A. Neevel
New Baltimore Reformed
 Church
John P. Newton
Harvey W. Noordsy
The Rev. Paul & Joan Nulton
Betty & Victor Nuovo
Michael P. Otte
Arthur E. Oudemool
Dr. Richard C. Oudersluys
Nolan Palsma
Donald S. Pangburn
George & Natalie Parry
Russell F. Pater
Thora H. Paton
Diana J. Paulsen
Darcy Lovgren Pavich
Richard A. Petrie
Elizabeth M. Pierce
Daniel Plasman
Richard F. Plechner
Dr. Louis P. Pojman
The Rev. Samuel H. Pomper
A. J. Poppen
Okke Postma

Bette Jane Poulos
The Rev. Linda & Mr. Stephen
  Powell
Iteke Prins
Aaron & Marlene Pulhamus
Perry Raak
Daniel Ramaker
The Rev. Karyn Ratcliffe & Mr.
  Chris Ratcliffe
Roland Ratmeyer
Jane Richardson
David Risseeuw
Louis Ruprecht
The Rev. Harold L Rutherford
William & Nancy Ryan
Dr. Leopold Schneider
Tom Schwanda
The Rev. Ernest Schwehm, III
Susanna Schweizer
Ms. Adrian L. Scott
The Rev. Carl Scovel
Dr. & Mrs. John C. Shetler
Harriet Sinclair
Dr. Richard R. Smyth
J. Matthew Soeter
The Rev. Louis O. Springsteen
Donald J. Stager
The Rev. Ronald C. Stockhoff
Sally B. Strong
LeRoy & Gerloa Suess
Dick Suffern
Pastor William B. Sutton, III

Shirley Taylor
Norman & Nancy Tellier
Mrs. Bard Thompson
Ian S. Todd
Robert & Helen Tulenko
Harry R. Tysen
The Rev. Dr. Walter J. Ungerer
United Reformed Church of
  Youngsville, NY
Kirk Vandersall
Dirk C. VanDerwerker
Merwin "Mike" Van Doornik
Gerard & Ruth Van Dyk
Arthur O. Van Eck
Tony Vis
Ruth Vogel
The Rev. H. Vogelaar
David & Janet Waanders
Mildred & Ted Wagner
Roy Wagoner
Florence & Peter Walker
The Rev. Kenneth L. Walsh
Paul & Deborah Walther
The Rev. Girdie B. Washington
The Rev. Dudley A. Webb
Richard Welscott
Ross Westhuis
Carol A. Whittaker
Beverly Bell Winslow
Stanley Yin
John & Anita Zavacky
Edith E. Zindle

Contents

Part II
Good Friday 1968 Sermons
The Seven Last Words

Part IV
Easter Sunday

Part VI
Pentecost Day

Acknowledgments

Following the publication of *In Remembrance and Hope, The Ministry and Vision of Howard G. Hageman,* I received considerable encouragement to publish some of Howard's sermons. Many of us knew Dr. Hageman as an eloquent and insightful preacher, and so I turned to Carol, Howard's wife of almost fifty years, for advice and assistance. From cellar and attic we retrieved box upon box of sermons. Although they were not filed systematically, almost every sermon, typed on Howard's old Remington manual typewriter, was accompanied by a church bulletin. As one may expect, this discovery added a colorful historical and geographical context for each and every manuscript.

With the careful and conscientious assistance of my daughter Katherine and Steven Hoffman, we catalogued the almost two thousand sermons on a computer spreadsheet which included text, date, location preached, and liturgical day or season. This organization has provided us with the remarkable ability to retrieve sermons easily by their biblical texts, from Genesis through Revelation. All the sermons were retyped by Steven Hoffman, a gift of time and skill for which I am deeply grateful. A special word of appreciation is extended to the Reverend Renee House, Gardner Sage Library, New Brunswick Theological Seminary, who not only provided the appropriate files and boxes for this project, but who has extended the hospitality of Gardner Sage as the location where Howard's sermons will be housed and made available for reading and research.

Finally, my deepest gratitude to Carol Hageman, who read every sermon and gently assisted in editing the spoken words of past decades into these written words for future generations. Carol brought to the task not only the enviable experience of having heard these sermons when they were preached, but the profound knowledge and love of the people who sat in the pews and received them as food for their journey of faith.

Gregg A. Mast
East Nassau, New York

Preface

Howard Hageman first came into my life at Central College in 1950 in a series of sermons preached for Religious Emphasis Week. Like many college students, I was involved in a crisis of faith. Howard's eloquence, erudition, and emphasis upon the living Christ put my doubts to flight.

In the reading of the manuscript for this volume, I was reminded again of the power of Howard's eloquence. His mastery of language, the creativity of thought, his honesty concerning the doubts of our age (which have only increased), all in the service of the good news of the living Christ, returned afresh. The sermons, even when preached in the context of contemporaneous crises, have a timeless quality as eternal as the gospel itself.

Howard was steeped in Scripture, and the sermons will soon reveal that he had been brought up on the King James Version of the Bible. So steeped in these Scriptures was Howard that Elizabethan English was quite naturally a part of his sermonic vocabulary. Our decision has been to allow Howard to speak with his own voice, for that voice resonated with Scripture. While having been a staunch advocate of the Revised Standard Version in the '40s and '50s, and while continuing to advocate the NRSV in the '90s, I must confess to a regret that the plethora of versions available has left few of today's clergy with a recognizable vocabulary of Scripture. Howard's voice is left as a challenge to all of us, even as his sermonic context continues as a challenge, paradigm, and resource to all who mount the pulpit.

The Reverend Dr. Gregg A. Mast has done a service to preachers everywhere by selecting sermons from the great days of the church year. These are precisely the days when many of us have asked, "What new message is there to preach? What words can I say that the congregation has not heard over and over again? Have these texts and themes not been preached on so often that through the repetition they now seemed worn and threadbare?" Howard's sermons for those days will come with a new vitality and originality from which present generations can continue to learn.

For Howard and his wife Carol, and to Gregg (who has known the power of these sermons) I, along with the church, express thanksgiving.

Donald J. Bruggink
General Editor

Introduction

As dusk was turning to darkness on the fourth Sunday of Advent, December 20, 1992, Howard Hageman died. His funeral was held at the North Reformed Church in Newark, New Jersey, where he had served for twenty-eight years as pastor. Some days later, a memorial service was celebrated at the old First Church in Albany, where as a young man he was introduced to the Dutch Reformed tradition. The lectionary reading for that Sunday was the familiar passage from the first chapter of the Gospel of John that includes the words: "In the beginning was the Word and the Word was with God, and the Word was God."

The Word and words were Howard's life. He read voraciously, he preached and taught with passion and eloquence, and he wrote extensively in a broad range of theological, historical, and liturgical areas. Howard loved words! Most important, Howard committed his life to discovering the Word among the words of the world. In 1977, he estimated he had preached in more than 250 congregations in the Reformed Church in America. By the time of his death, he had graced the pulpits of almost one-third of the churches. Yet, in spite of his widely acclaimed role as the favorite choice to preach anniversary and special celebration services, Howard did not write a great deal about preaching.

In 1952 Howard was invited to preach at the General Synod meeting, and he chose his text from 1 Thessalonians: "When ye received the Word of God which ye heard of us, ye received it not as the word of men, but, as it is in truth, the Word of God...." It is from the body of this sermon that we learn a great deal about Howard's theology of the Word that inspired his preaching:

> If we are to be more than talking shops, lecture halls, schools of doctrine, if we are to be fellowships of living power, then one of our desperate needs is to recover a right sense of what it means to preach and to hear the Word. I cannot but think that one of the most pernicious things that has happened to us in this regard is the exclusive way in which we have come to identify the Word of God with the Bible. Let there be no mistaking it; the Bible is the Word of God, but neither in a primary nor in an exclusive sense. How can we forget that primarily the Word of God is He that became flesh and dwelt among us, full of grace and truth, who still lives at the right hand of His Father? Any attempt to replace his primary position by a book stands condemned as idolatry.[1]

This clear and emphatic defense of a Christocentric view of preaching led Howard finally to confess the sacramental dimension of the pulpit. Indeed if he could have unilaterally declared preaching the third sacrament, he would have done it. Sermons are more than lectures about the Bible, or even opportunities to do biblical exegesis in a public setting, but the place and the time when the Christ comes again to live among us and within us. Preaching is the act of identifying the presence of the Word in our midst and listening closely to where he calls us to go, what he calls us to do, and, most important, who he calls us to be. Howard had not always

---

1   Howard G. Hageman, "Preaching the Word," *Church Herald* (September 19, 1952): 5.

held such a high view of preaching. He once confessed that in the early years of his career the pulpit was primarily understood by preachers as a place and time for the education of the congregation. He wrote: "This writer has destroyed his first sermons because they were really biblical and theological lectures, fairly well done 'head trips' but little else."[2] Howard went on to recall with some horror the first sermon he preached on Trinity Sunday in the early 1940s when he attempted to explain all the Athanasian mysteries in fifteen minutes!

His critical eye did not only turn toward his own work, but also toward a church that he feared had often lost the resolve to preach life's changing messages of resurrection. Howard was fond of quoting Ralph Waldo Emerson's description of the Reverend Barzillal Frost, the minister of the church Emerson attended in Concord. In Emerson's diary entry for March 18, 1838, a stormy, snowy day, these words appear:

> At church all day, but almost tempted to say I would go no more. Men go where they want to go, else had no soul gone this afternoon. The snowstorm was real; the preacher merely spectral. Vast contrast to look at him and then out of the window. He had no word intimating that he had ever laughed or wept, was married or enamored, had been cheated, or voted for or chagrined. If he had ever lived or acted, we were none the wiser for it.[3]

What the entry emphasizes is the lack of flesh and blood in the young preacher's sermon. For Howard, preaching was the opportunity to share the real presence of Christ. He shuddered when he heard preaching which would talk about God as an object of our study rather than the subject of our love and devotion. Preaching is not talking abut faith, but creating faith. It is not talking

2 Howard G. Hageman, "Preaching is Alive and Well," *Theology Today* 37 (January, 1981): 493-97.
3 "On Being A Real Parson," May 18, 1978, Hageman Collection, Gardner Sage Library, New Brunswick Theological Seminary, New Brunswick, New Jersey.

about the resurrection, but raising the dead. The pulpit is finally a place where one person speaks of the pain and joy of an entire congregation and the word of hope and challenge God has already spoken in the life of a carpenter.

In a lecture Howard apparently delivered at New Brunswick in 1984 entitled, "The Spirituality of John Calvin," he shared what he believed to be the understanding of preaching in the writings of the great reformer. It is interesting that Calvin never identified a separate place for the lesson in his liturgies, because the reading and the preaching of the Word were the same act. To highlight some important aspects of Calvin's theology of preaching, Howard used a brief portion of the lecture to analyze the following prayer, which Calvin used before the word.

> As we look into the face of the Son, Jesus Christ, our Lord, whom (God) has appointed Mediator between himself and us, let us beseech him in whom is all fullness of wisdom and light to vouchsafe to guide us by his Holy Spirit into the true understanding of his holy doctrine, making it productive in us of all the fruits of righteousness.[4]

Howard suggests we see in this prayer the real presence of Christ who comes to us in the preached Word through the power of the Holy Spirit. In response to being in the presence of the living Christ, our understanding of him is enlarged so that we may produce fruits of righteousness. It is immediately clear to the reader that these insights can be applied equally to the celebration of the sacrament of the Lord's Supper. Howard's suggestion is that the church needs to embrace the sacramental quality of preaching that is eloquently illustrated in this brief commentary on Calvin's prayer.

I suppose it is possible for the reader to assume that Howard had a minimalist view of Scripture, considering his high regard for the identification of the Word with the person of Christ. Nothing could

---

4 Bard Thompson, *Liturgies of the Western Church* (Cleveland: The World Publishing Company, 1982), 209.

be further from the truth! For Howard, a sermon without its biblical moorings often was carried into the uncharted waters of the preacher's imagination and private theology. He described this as the great failure of the liberal church. He also criticized the conservative church as simply reciting biblical material as proof for theological propositions.

"We need to remind ourselves," he wrote, "that Calvin was not afraid of the equation, *Predicatio Verbi Dei est Verbum Dei* (the preaching of the Word of God is the Word of God)."[5] Such a high view of preaching meant that Howard assumed the task of preaching with the utmost seriousness. The preacher's first responsibility, according to Howard, is to read all the lections for the week and to listen and look for that word or text that catches his or her attention. Once the text is selected then the preacher is called to do the homework of a homilitician. Commentaries and lives must be read and savored. The interaction between the text and the congregation is crucial. If a preacher does not know his people, then the great risk is that the preacher, who is not quite a real person, will speak to a congregation filled with not quite real people about not quite real things.

In 1969, Howard dedicated part of his column to a parish paper produced by a Reformed congregation in Rotterdam. The Dutch newsletter included an inspiring piece written by a lay person in response to the question, "What do I expect from our ministers in the pulpit?" After focusing on the corporate dimension of preaching, the author concluded with these words:

> Then the sermon will be the point at which the vertical line (which comes from God) touches the horizontal line (which comes from us). A real flash of lightning! Sunday church-going then becomes an event, something which always remains open and free. But seen this way, the

5 Howard G. Hageman, "The Need and Promise of Reformed Preaching," *Church Herald* (October 17, 1975): 6.

congregation is just as much responsible for the sermon as the dominie....[6]

The weekly interaction between the preacher and congregation is the time to let the text "simmer" on the back burner of the preacher's mind and soul. In Howard's own preparation, he moved from exegetical study to writing the entire sermon in a single sentence by Wednesday morning. This discipline saved him countless hours of wandering the theological landscape when he finally put his hand to writing. He spent the rest of the week collecting his thoughts and insights on small cards and pieces of paper that he would empty onto his desk at the time of his Saturday composition. "Because you have been living with the text all week, talking to it, arguing with it, looking for it, most of the materials which you need are going to be there," he writes.[7]

It was his personal discipline to write every sermon he preached. Realizing that there are many preachers who bristle at such a routine, Howard observed that for him "good craftsmanship demands the discipline of writing." As he organized each sermon, he attempted ruthlessly to excise everything that did not address the central idea. This homiletical mode produced a structure that was clear and clean in its lines. Although a congregation may not in the end agree with what a preacher has shared, it is crucial that they know what he or she has said, Howard observed. Finally the choice of language is crucial to the enterprise because a congregation must see what it hears.

Having followed Howard through a normal week of sermon preparation, we need to catch a glimpse of him in the pulpit. He was considered by many to be one of the finest preachers of the latter half of the twentieth century. Howard was as dramatic in the pulpit as he was quietly self-deprecating out of it. He gestured with hands

6 Howard G. Hageman, "A Layman Looks At Preaching," *Church Herald* (February 28, 1969): 9.
7 Howard G. Hageman, "Preaching is Alive and Well," *Theology Today* 37 (January, 1981): 493-97.

which literally directed the symphony of words. I often thought of a great thunderstorm rumbling across a lake as an image of his finely honed voice. Each sentence would begin gently and build as it reached its crescendo. In and through it all, the congregation had an abiding sense that this preacher believed what he was saying. Sermons, for Howard, had to come from an intersection between the Word and the world. The situation had to exegete the Word as the Word interpreted the world. It was Isaac Da Costa, the Dutch leader in the religious movements who finally prompted Albertus van Raalte to come to Michigan and Hendrik Scholte to Iowa, who wrote: "When you prepare a sermon, put your newspaper next to your Bible." As we move to consider the work of the sermon after its delivery, Howard was fond of quoting B. A. Gerrish, a modern Reformation scholar, who once observed:

> (Luther) preached the Word, slept, and drank beer; and while he did nothing more, the Word did it all. With Calvin things were quite different. As he lay on his deathbed, he fell to reminiscing about the course of his life and remarked: "When I first arrived in this church, there was almost nothing. They were preaching and that is all. There was no reformation.[8]

For Howard, the act of preaching and worship can be seen poetically in the walk of two disciples along the Emmaus road. Into the midst of their crucified lives a stranger appears and shares with them all that the scriptures had to say to their buried hopes. As importantly, the stranger becomes known to them in breaking bread, which prompts these weary travelers to run back down the same Emmaus road to share new life. There is no place in the story for the disciples to sit back and rest secure in their private knowledge of the resurrection. The work of Easter is the work of helping

---

8 Brian Gerrish, *The Old Protestantism and the New* (Chicago: University of Chicago Press, 1982), 109.

change the world into the new creation. The pulpit and the preacher are at the cutting edge of that divine task.

Howard often lauded the Roman church for its recovery of an appreciation of preaching in its life, as he called the Protestant tradition to move toward a parallel recovery of the sacraments in our ecclesiastical life. Howard was convinced that first the Reformed church needed to understand and appreciate the sacramental nature of preaching. He asked, "How can we talk about the real presence of Christ in the breaking of bread if we have not first been made aware of the real presence of Christ in the preaching of the Word?"[9]

J. D. Benoit, a French liturgical scholar, put the challenge in this way:

> This, it seems to me, is the great lack in our preaching; it does not nourish souls. It does not take them by the hand, so to speak, and bring them to God, but always leaves them in the same situation, that of the morning after confirmation....It does not address itself to their spiritual development. It is the pastor who must distribute the bread which makes our souls live and grow spiritually.[10]

It is to that challenge that Howard wrote and preached. It was to that challenge that Howard called the church to wrestle with God in a time when people all too often live a life of quiet desperation. Howard loved to quote Francis Thompson, who wrote not only the well-known poem, "The Hound of Heaven," but also a smaller poem that he entitled, "The Kingdom of God," with the subtitle, "In No Strange Land." A few lines call us to the task of the pulpit and the pew:

> O world invisible, we view thee,

---

9 Howard G. Hageman, "Sacramental Seriousness," *Reformed Journal* 35 No.3 (March, 1985): 4.

10 J. D. Benoit, "Les Deficits de la Predication" (an address delivered at the synod of the Reformed Church of Alsace-Lorraine, September 1952), 4-5.

O world intangible, we touch thee,
O world unknowable, we know thee,
Inapprehensible, we clutch thee....

The angels keep their ancient places;
Turn but a stone, and start a wing!
'Tis ye, 'Tis your estranged faces
That miss the many splendored thing....

Yea in the night, my soul, my daughter,
Cry—clinging heaven by the hems:
And lo, Christ walking on the water
Not of Gennesaret, but Thames![11]

Gregg A. Mast
East Nassau, New York

Originally published as, "The Pulpit: In the Beginning Was the Word," in Gregg A. Mast, In Remembrance and Hope, *(Grand Rapids, Michigan: Wm. B. Eerdmans Publishing Co., 1998), 12-19.*

11 Howard G. Hageman, "In No Strange Land," *Princeton Seminary Bulletin* 68 (Autumn, 1975): 51.

Part I

We Call This Friday Good, 1961.

The Seven Last Words

These sermons were originally preached to the congregation of the North Reformed Church in Newark, New Jersey. They were published in 1961: Howard G. Hageman, We Call This Friday Good, *(Philadelphia, Pennsylvania: Muhlenberg Press, 1961)*

1

We Call This Friday Good

But where sin abounded,
grace did much more abound.
    Romans 5:20

... and that is why we call this Friday good!

We use the phrase, "Good Friday," so often that it does not puzzle us, principally because we never think about it. "Good Friday" is a stereotyped kind of phrase.

But surely someone who knew nothing at all of the facts of our faith, who had no previous acquaintance with its meaning, hearing the story of this Friday would wonder exactly why we chose to call it "good." Whether you have any religious inclinations or not, it is surely strange to take a day on which an innocent man was brutally murdered, a day in which the power of justice was turned upside down and the forces of religion went blind, and label it for all future history *Good* Friday. What kind of inverted logic is that anyway? What is so good about judicial murder? What is so good about physical pain and agony? What is so good about innocent suffering and unmerited death?

Yes, if our questioner knew just a little bit about American history and recalled that once upon a time in Wall Street there was a Friday in which fortunes were wiped out, large companies bankrupted, countless people deprived of their life savings, our questioner might well wonder about our standard of values that we should call the Friday marked by financial ruin "black," while the Friday marked by history's most terrible murder is known as "good."

Well, why do we call this Friday good? I hope that no one thinks it is for sentimental or piously romantic reasons. We call this Friday good because it was on this Friday that the truth expressed by St. Paul was specifically and sublimely guaranteed. "Where sin abounded, grace did much more abound." That remark, of course, is more than a casual observation. It is an entire life-view, a whole world-faith. Those eight short words by themselves form a creed of gigantic proportions. For they assert that the greatest power that you and I can find in this world is the power of God's love.

Is that really true? Can we believe it, be sure of it, live by it? The Christian gospel replies that it was made certain at Calvary this Friday ... and that is why we call this Friday good!

No one who studied the scene will want to deny, I am sure, that there at the cross sin certainly abounded. But it abounded not in grossness and vulgarity; it abounded in refinement and decency. That's what makes the scene there at Calvary so terrifying. If our Lord had fallen into the hands of a pack of rascals, a gang of thugs, if he had been victimized by some hoodlums or muggers like those who infest our city streets, that would have been bad enough. But in its way it would have been understandable.

But the hands into which he fell were the clean hands, the politely washed hands of society's most respected members—ministers, lawyers, politicians, industrialists, college professors, intellectuals. I shall not linger over so familiar a scene, nor do I need to prove that at the cross sin abounded. I want simply to call to mind the fact that it abounded because there at the cross it was at its most subtle and sinister best, not wearing the lurid colors of low crime and dark passion, but the somber and respectable shades of rationality, decency, orderliness, compromise.

No, it was not the women of the street, the degenerates with throats aflame with thirst, the racketeers, gangsters, and extortioners who nailed Christ to his cross. It was the nice people, the quiet, peace-loving, stable people. That's why sin abounded. It had succeeded in so blinding the minds of the best people in the community that they had no idea that they were sinning.

Did grace much more abound? Did God's love prove the master of that terrible situation? I think we must be careful how we answer for we are such creatures of time and space that we think when the things of time and space are lost, all is lost. It would be easy for us to be honest, to turn away from this heart-rending scene and say, "No, sin abounded! He died. There was none to help, none to deliver, none to save."

But there are more important tragedies than the tragedy of death, more important victories than the victory of deliverance. Did his faith fail him? No. Did his love grow cold and bitter? No. Did his spirit turn sour and ugly? No. Did his vision fail, his hope perish? No. Then *where sin abounded, grace did much more abound*. For in everything in life that really matters, the love of God proved stronger than the brutality of humanity.

And if you step back from the foot of the cross and look down through the centuries, you will see it all the more clearly. Why do people gather on that same Friday more than nineteen hundred years later? To mourn the death of a loved one? Hardly; sorrow is more quickly forgotten by most of us; we do not mourn for nineteen centuries. Or more pointedly, why is that same cross set at the central point in thousands upon thousands of Christian churches? As a kind of tombstone to say, "Here he died"? Not at all—but as the everlasting witness that here the love of God and the sin of man tried their strength and the love of God conquered!

> Love of God, O sin of man,
> In this dread act your strength is tried.
> And victory remains with Love!
> Jesus, my Lord, is crucified.

But surely it is more than the significance of this one day that holds our hearts. It is something to know why we call this Friday good, I grant you, for one cannot really explain it without touching on the innermost heart of our believing. But, if I may put it this way, the even more glorious truth is that this man, this cross, this God have the power to make all our Fridays good. It is not just that one Friday, one dark spot in human history, was redeemed and set aglow, but that the love of God is always redeeming love which can make all Fridays good, which can make all difficulties, trials, and sufferings things of meaning, beauty, and strength.

"Where sin abounded, grace did much more abound" is, I know, a statement in the past tense. But it has a present and it has a future. God's love is always greater than your worst difficulties. God's love shall always be greater than your bitterest need. I know that there are times when all of us would give a good deal to be able to answer the question of why sin abounds. There are many times when we wonder why it abounds in a personal way, spreading its poison through our lives almost without our knowing it or willing it.

But not only that, there are more times when we wonder why it abounds so that even when we are innocent, the sin of others reaches out to involve us. There is nothing more disheartening than the discovery that no one sins privately, but that all of us drag into the mire even those whom we love best. Why should the world be like that? Why should one little sin which is mine and for which I am willing to pay spread to taint the lives of twenty other people? Why does sin abound?

People must have wondered about that as they watched that innocent man die that first Good Friday. They got no answer. You and I will get none either. Or rather, we shall get an answer, but not to the question we are asking. God's love is more abundant and more powerful than sin. It turns defeats into victories, black Fridays into good ones, dark valleys into havens of light, suffering into strength, crosses into shrines. This Good Friday when we look at his cross we must think about it in these positive terms. We can take all of our problems, all of our sorrows, all of our temptations, all of our failures, all of the things that get us down, put them in the balances, and his cross will outweigh them all.

This was the joyful discovery of the pioneers of the Christian faith. This has been the same joyful discovery of all those who have found it again and again as age has succeeded age. The gospel is not here to discuss what ought to be, but what is. And what is in our lives is still sin, suffering, trouble, foolish ventures, tragic failures. The gospel is not here to scold and say that they never should have taken place. That's no help. We know that now.

Nor is it here simply to say that they can vanish as though they had never been. It is here to declare that the love of God is so great that it can take whatever you have and redeem it into something good. Your sin can become your strength. Your problem can become your song. Your suffering can become new faith, your loneliness can become new love, not by any magic, but by the power of God's love shown at the cross. That love can make every Friday good.

And so we shall sit at the foot of the cross for another Good Friday. We shall not be watching the unfolding of some tragic scene or listening to the dying words of a martyr. We shall be learning how God's love works through human weakness, failure, and sin, bringing light and love, peace and joy.

... and that is why we call this Friday good!

2

The First Word

Father, forgive them;
for they know not what they do.
    Luke 23:34

Now the teaching of Jesus ceases to be theory and becomes reality. In the Sermon on the Mount our Lord commands us to love our enemies; on the cross he obeys his own command. In the Sermon on the Mount our Lord tells us to do good to those who use us spitefully; on the cross he follows his own teaching. In the Sermon on the Mount our Lord instructs us that forgiveness is the hallmark of discipleship; on the cross he illustrates his own instruction.

I have often thought that if I had any doubt as to the divinity of Jesus Christ, this would be the place at which it would be resolved. I can see how one might doubt Jesus in spite of his virgin birth. I can understand how one might examine the record of his miracles and yet not be convinced of his deity. But I cannot understand how anyone could go to the foot of his cross, listen to this word of forgiveness, and not confess with the pagan captain who was in charge of the crucifixion, "Truly, this was the Son of God."

8

For myself, whenever I hear these words in their context of exquisite agony of soul and excruciating pain of body, I know that I am hearing something which no purely human voice could speak, so far do they transcend the love and the goodness that are in my heart or that would be in my heart under similar circumstances. That our Lord could and did speak them not only convinces me that he was the Son of God, but it heartens me to know that the kind of God proclaimed in the Christian gospel is one who even in the torment of crucifixion could say, "Forgive."

Yes, the more I think about it, the more it seems to me that this first word from the cross is a kind of creed, small in size, but tremendous in what it comprehends. For here in this one sentence is the Christian understanding of God and the Christian understanding of humanity. And I should like to begin at what may seem the wrong end. I should like to begin with what this word has to say about us, so that we may understand in sharper outline and clearer detail what it has to say about God.

Have you ever been puzzled about the meaning of the second part of this first word from the cross, "They know not what they do"? To whom was our Lord referring? Where can you draw the line? Did he simply ask forgiveness for the soldiers who must do their duty and go through this bloody business of crucifixion, even though they had no understanding of its moral meaning? Can you limit his forgiveness that narrowly?

Did he also ask forgiveness for the priests, the scribes and Pharisees, whose jealous plotting had produced this terrible result, since they did not foresee to what a frightful end their scheming would lead? Can you in all conscience set any limits to the application of this word? Does it not rather reach out to include all of us so that for you and me, five thousand miles and two thousand years away from the actual event, Jesus Christ is still praying, "Father, forgive them; for they know not what they do"?

Well, if you agree (and I do not see how you can stop the meaning of this word at anything less), then I challenge you to consider what a revelation of human nature is contained in these words, "They know not what they do." It was Plato, I think, who first argued a case which has been taken up many times since, that what we call sin is in point of fact simple ignorance, that the reason why we do wrong is simply that we do not know what is right. It was Plato's conclusion, therefore, that the only effective remedy for wrongdoing is education. If you want people to do right, then you must teach them what is right.

Well, it does not take much intelligence to see that the theory is too simple and that the problem is not nearly so easy. In some instances, to be sure, we may sin from ignorance, we may do things which we would not do if we knew better. But in many more instances that is not true. With perfect intellectual understanding of what we ought to do, we do what we know we ought not to do. Ignorance may excuse a boy from the slums who steals a loaf of bread. But the member of a church who gossips maliciously about a neighbor does not have ignorance as an excuse. No, there are just too many things that we do knowingly and deliberately to allow us to beg off responsibility by saying, "We didn't know."

But then, was our Lord mistaken when he said from his cross, "They know not what they do"? Perhaps the soldiers were acting in ignorance. But the priests, the scribes and Pharisees, the mob, you, me—all of whom he is certainly ready to forgive—can you say that they, or we, did what was done in ignorance? I hardly think so.

And yet I hardly think that our Lord was wrong about human nature either. There is an ignorance of the mind which makes mistakes because it lacks information. And that ignorance we can remedy. But that is not the ignorance our Lord is talking about here. For there is a deeper ignorance of the soul which arises not from lack of information, but from lack of proper direction, attitude, and inner motive. And from that ignorance, no matter what may have been our schooling, we all suffer. In the deepest and most tragic sense of the word, "We know not what we do."

Here is our Lord's dying observation about human nature—its sheer stupidity. You can follow it out in a number of directions. Let me suggest two. Because of our tragic ignorance of soul, our twisted motives, our warped attitudes, we do not know what we are and therefore inevitably we do not know what we do. How easily I think that I am the axis on which the universe revolves, so that, without meaning to be proud or demanding, I expect life to meet my terms. And because I am easily the most important and interesting thing that I know, I can do the crudest and the cruelest things to gain my ends, without ever thinking of them as crude, or realizing their cruelty. I can always justify in my own conduct what I would be quick to condemn in yours.

Every Lent we heap reproach on the Jewish priesthood for what it did in crucifying Christ. And yet, if you could have interviewed Annas or Caiaphas the day after Good Friday, either of those reverend gentlemen could have given you a perfectly rational explanation for his conduct, one in which he himself would have sincerely believed. And what is more, had I been in the high priest's robes, I should doubtless have done the same thing with the same conviction that I was right. We have lost all sense of proportion in the universe. We do not know what we do because we do not know who we are. And we generally crucify those who try to tell us.

I think of a second aspect of this ignorance of soul. I am always amazed at what little awareness people have of the contagious quality of wrongdoing—until I stop to consider how little awareness I have of it myself! If I want to hate you, I think that's my business. But I am so wrong! Once I release the poison of hatred, it has a way of spreading where I can no longer control it. Have you never seen an entire group poisoned because just two persons had a private quarrel? Have you never known an organization cleft into hostile camps because just two persons disliked each other?

Well, here is the reason which, in our ignorance of soul, we overlook. My sin is never *my* sin. Like a cancer, it will eat its way through any society, any group, any family of which I am part. Once it has started, I can no more stop it than I can tell its final destination. Judas's desire for a fast thirty pieces of silver ends with the crucifixion of his master. *I didn't know.* A man's infatuation with another woman ends in the ruin of his innocent children. *I didn't know.* Of course they didn't; not that they lacked the education, the head to understand, but they lacked the heart. That is our human situation and if we get no further than recognizing it, we shall have taken a giant step forward. Not because our information is poor, but because our minds are warped, our hearts are hard, our wills are weak, we do not know what we do.

But we can get further than that because this first word from the cross, this little creed, contains another affirmation, *Father, forgive them.* If ignorance of soul be our Lord's verdict on human nature, here is his final belief about God: "Father, forgive." The two words belong together, do they not? It is because God is a father that his very nature is forgiveness. And it is because forgiveness is the most basic experience that we can have with God that you and I can say "our Father."

How do we know that God is our Father? Not just because in some vague way he created us and endowed us with life, but because time and again when we come back from the strange ways of our ignorance and stupidity, we find him waiting for us with a welcoming heart. And how do we find the courage—the nerve, if you like—to come to God and ask his forgiveness after what we have been and what we have done? Because we have been persuaded that the heart of the Eternal is the heart of a Father.

I recall a friend from university days, the victim of rather a tragic personal life, who told me he was not a Christian because there was one statement in the Apostles' Creed in which he could not believe. I supposed it would be the virgin birth or the resurrection of the body, things which quite often cause difficulty in intellectual circles. I was all set to give him an enthusiastic argument. But I was completely unprepared for what he said. "No, it is not those things that stop me. I cannot believe in the forgiveness of sins."

You know, I think there are thousands like him. Even though they may profess their faith in the forgiveness of sins, they do it in a purely mechanical and formal way, without realizing, without ever realizing that here is one of the most triumphant assertions our creed has to make. When I think of the people who are tied in knots by the chains of their past mistakes, when I consider the people who keep nursing the sores of old quarrels, opening the wounds of old battles, when I think how all of us let ourselves be dominated by what we have been rather than by what we could be, then I wish for the tongue of an angel to convince you and myself that the bedrock reality of this world and the next is a Father who forgives.

The Lord Christ affirmed this during all the years of his ministry among us, and not even the sharpness of death could make him change his mind about it. Blind and stupid creatures that we are, we do not have to suffer the penalties of our blindness, the results of our stupidity. We do not have to let life be frustrated and defeated by the silly mistakes and selfish sins with which we spoil it. For if the truth about us be that we are badly mistaken about ourselves that we do everything backward, the truth about God is that he will forgive and forget the whole wretched record, giving us not only any number of new chances, but the grace to make those chances good.

Indeed, here is the best way to make this Friday good—to let these two truths stand out in all their stark reality till they have driven their way deep into our lives. Now is the time to stop fooling ourselves about ourselves, now is the time for self-examination. And what self-examination is worthy of the name that does not reveal ourselves to ourselves, as we are, all sham and pretense gone? But now is also the time in which with unclouded vision we see God as he is and are brought to a new awareness of the rich resources in him whom we generally treat so casually and think of so mistakenly.

And here in the first word from the cross is the answer to our searchings—the brutal truth about ourselves and the glorious truth about God. If you see only the brutal truth about human nature, you can easily become despairing and cynical. If you see only the glorious truth about God, you can easily assume a false optimism and a light responsibility. But if you see both, the full extent of our ignorance mastered by the fuller extent of God's love, then you can hang on a cross and still keep faith!

Father, forgive them; for they know not what they do. There we are, you and I, as we are. And there is God as he is, eternally. And to be able to say words like these, even from a cross—there are you and I as Christ can make us!

3

The Second Word

Verily I say unto thee,
Today shalt thou be with me in paradise.
    Luke 23:43

I doubt that there is a character in all the pages of the New Testament who has been the subject of more speculation and more romancing than this penitent thief who hung in death with our Lord. Actually, all that we know about him is contained in this single incident, recorded only in St. Luke's Gospel. But pious legend has given him a name, Dismas, and pious speculation, endeavoring to find the reason for his eleventh-hour discovery of Christ, has built up whole biographies of him.

But the fact is that whoever or whatever he was, so far as history is concerned he appears only for this one unforgettable moment. He had probably been an assassin, a political revolutionary. The chances are that he and his companion in crucifixion had been associates of that celebrated rebel Barabbas who had been released that very morning at the behest of the mob.

I do not pretend to know what suddenly prompted a change of heart on the part of this man whose entire life had been one of

15

violence and murder, who, very likely, had never so much as seen
Jesus Christ until they were led out together to die. I suspect that it
may have been that he too heard that first word from the cross,
"Father, forgive them; for they know not what they do," and that
such an unusual cry in this place of cursing and pain had started him
wondering and thinking. At any rate, like the character in Shakespeare,
nothing in his life became him like the leaving of it. For out of the
darkness on Calvary, his is the next voice that we hear in an
unforgettable request. "Lord, remember me when thou comest
into thy kingdom."

Our Lord's reply is usually interpreted to mean that it is never too
late to turn to him in faith and repentance. Here is a man whose
entire career, we may safely assume, has been godless and wicked.
And in the last hours of his life by a single change of heart he leaves
the hell of which, up to that point, he had never even heard. Down
to the end of the end, down to life's last breath, the possibility of
paradise is there for all who will repent and believe, no matter what
their previous record. Like St. Augustine they may complain, "Too
late have I loved thee, O beauty old, yet ever new! Too late have I
loved thee!" They may complain, and rightly so, of all that they have
missed in not coming to their senses sooner. But never can they
complain that, though they came late, they were excluded. If this
second word from the cross says anything, it says that with Jesus
Christ there is never a "too late."

Now that, I say, is the common and obvious interpretation of this
episode. And if I spend no more time with it, it is not because I do
not believe it to be true. It is rather because it is so obvious that we
all see it and accept it and can go on, therefore, to consider some
things which are not so common and obvious but of great importance
for us nonetheless.

And the first thing I would notice is that here is a magnificent
illustration of the way in which God's greatness exceeds our
expectations. The request of the penitent thief had been, after all,
a rather indefinite one. Remember me. He had not asked for

anything in particular. He had not, like two of our Lord's own disciples, asked for some special place of honor in this kingdom which was to come. He had not even asked to be let off from any penalty he might have to pay for the kind of life he had lived.

Nor was he, as is so often suggested, trying to evade whatever destiny justice would assign him in another world. His simple request was that he might not be forgotten in that other world, that this man next to him in death, who, events had convinced him, would be lord of that other world, would not forget these hours of pain when his crucified companion had recognized even in his dying something of his glory. "Sir, remember me."

It was a very modest request. But look at the response! "Today shalt thou be with me in paradise." Not, "I'll remember you," which is all anyone could have expected under the circumstances, but an answer that in every possible way was far more than anyone could have imagined. Not, "I'll remember you when I come into my kingdom," but *today*. You will not have to wait for your request to be answered; it will not be postponed to some distant future, but *today*.

And not, "Today will I remember you, as you have asked, letting some dim recollection of your speaking to me influence my decisions about you." But, "Today you will be with me. I will not only remember you; I will take you with me." And not, "Today you will be with me on the beautiful isle of somewhere," some vague uncertain spot, but in paradise, in that place of unclouded joy and undimmed hope which God has prepared for those who love him.

I go into such detail because I am convinced that here we have not a peculiar incident standing by itself but one which is just as applicable to us as to the thief on the cross. I suspect that most of us would have to acknowledge or complain about the poverty of our spiritual lives. We do not have the triumphant faith, the victorious love, the invincible courage, the undying hope we should like to have. There is something so drab and ordinary about our religion.

Now you can think of as many reasons for that unhappy situation as I can. But here is one of which you may not have thought. We don't expect enough. We consistently underestimate what God can do, or is willing to do. If there are some Christians who are guilty of exaggerating the claims of their religion, ours is the reverse fault: we are always writing them down.

Once in a Sunday school class I asked, "Do you think that God is as close to people today as he was in Bible times?" It was the opinion of almost all the young people in the class that he was not, an opinion for which, incidentally, I should not blame them at all. If they observe the religious behavior of their elders, to what other conclusion could they come? The New Testament is filled with magnificent promises: in all these things we are more than conquerors; we sit together in the heavenly places with Christ Jesus; we are filled with all the fullness of God, and so the triumphant chorus goes. But we spend our time trying to show that these words don't really mean us, instead of reaching out in high expectancy to claim what is already ours in the goodness of God.

The clear lesson of the gospel is that for every one thing for which we ask, God is willing and ready to give us three. Ask to be remembered and you gain paradise! But we don't ask. We scrape together such little faith as can be shaved off life's edges. We dare such little hope as will never make us disappointed. We cultivate the little love we have left from life's more pressing relationships. And with such miserable equipment we limp through life, battered and bruised by its events, but still saying wisely, "There is nothing in the claims of Christianity."

One of our poets has said that God answers us not by the measure of our asking but by the measure of God's munificence. But alas, most of us know God not by the measure of his munificence, but by the measure of our own timidity and skepticism. And for that reason most of us have not even begun to realize what possibilities there are for us in God. If a dying thief could ask simply to be remembered and then be granted paradise, what might not you and

I obtain if we asked our Father, who is able to do exceeding abundantly more than we can ask or think, through Jesus Christ our Lord.

But in this whole matter of asking and receiving, there is a still more specific factor which I am tempted to call the time factor. I observe that we have a way of evading the gifts of God's goodness not only by underestimating them but by postponing them to a far-off future. Thus when we read in St. Paul that death is swallowed up in victory, we think only of the final resurrection, ages and ages away. When we read in the gospels about eternal life, we immediately connect it with something we shall receive when we die.

We do it all along the line. It is perfectly amazing how we have made of the New Testament, no more than a small part of which deals with the future, something that has almost its chief relevance in the future, and not too certain a future at that. The crucified thief shared our way of thinking. Lord, remember me when thou comest into thy kingdom. No telling when that might be or when he thought it would be. But he did not expect it soon if for no other reason than that crucified daydreamers do not overnight become kings with kingdoms! It was the future—the distant future—which the penitent thief had in mind when he spoke.

But now again, look at the reply. "Today shalt thou be with me in paradise." What had been hoped for the future is here as a present possibility. You can, of course, reply that since both the thief and Jesus Christ were about to leave this life, it would have to be that very day that they were together in paradise. But this misses the point. Let me put it this way. If these same words had been spoken by our Lord to the penitent thief at a time and place when each of them still had fifty years to live, they would have meant the same. For these words do not refer so much to the place to which they were going, by virtue of their common death, as to the new relationship into which they had entered by reason of faith. "To be with me in paradise" is not primarily a promise for the future but a possibility for the present.

For to be with Jesus Christ, whenever and wherever it takes place, is to be in paradise. It is an experience that doubtless will become more perfect and complete when we have passed beyond the limitations of this mortal life. But that does not preclude its beginning here within the limitations of this mortal life. Heaven, as we call it, is not a totally distinct realm from earth into which we shall be translated by the fact of death. It is an experience which interpenetrates the experiences of our mortality. There is no heaven, no paradise possible in another world for those who have not begun, however imperfectly, their experience of it here.

The dying thief did not begin his experience of paradise after he had drawn his last breath in this world. He began it at the moment he recognized in his dying companion the Lord and master of his life. And when his spirit left his body for that other world, it was simply to go on in greater realization of something which had already, though for a very short time, been begun here.

Now, lest you think I am spinning fancies and neglecting reality, let me hasten briefly to illustrate what I mean. I mean that it is possible even in the contradictions and confusions of this life to keep the center of your being calm and undisturbed. I mean that it is possible even in this life to go through one hellish situation after another with strength and confidence of spirit. I mean that it is possible to endure physical pain and suffering while the mind and heart are filled with peace and joy. That's what I mean by being in paradise even while you are still part of this earthly scene of chance and change.

And I know that it is life's most glorious possibility—possible only when we are there with Christ. It is Jesus' presence in our lives that makes paradise possible even on a cross. For, while I would be the last in the world to minimize those good things which God has prepared for them that love him, none of us needs to sit mooning and pining for their coming when the most heavenly possibilities are available to us right here and now.

Those who live victoriously, though they wait in great hope and expectation for the final triumph of God's grace, live even more in present experience of what that grace in Christ can do in their lives here and now. *Today shalt thou be with me in paradise* is no idle promise for an indefinite future but a simple statement of what Christ can and will do here and now if we put our trust in him and open our lives to his presence and power.

And that, of course, is the tragedy and the glory of the penitent thief. His tragedy is that his introduction to paradise came so late. If only he had met our Lord two or three years earlier, what hell he might have been spared, from what defeats he would have been delivered, from what fears he would have been saved, what mistakes he would have avoided. And his glory is that he found Jesus in time, not only to win eternity, but to gain strength of spirit and faith even in the agony of his cross.

His tragedy and his glory are not unlike yours and mine. And Good Friday is the opportunity to redeem tragedy into glory. For what is our tragedy but our failure to grasp what Christ can do for our lives here and now? And what is our glory but to discover with him how to live in heaven even while we are still on earth?

4

The Third Word

Woman, behold thy son!
...Behold thy mother!
    John 19:26-27

There is something very human and appealing about this third word from the cross. Perhaps it does not blind us with the brilliance of its glory like the word which came before it. Perhaps it does not shake us to the depths of our being like that searching cry which will follow it. But in its human tenderness it has a quality all its own.

Sometime after his conversation with the penitent thief, our Lord looked down from his cross and saw his mother standing at his feet in the company of several other women and the disciple whom he loved. I must underscore the fact that the evangelist says deliberately that Mary was *standing* at the foot of the cross. She was not swooning or carrying on, indulging herself in some emotional display, but standing in all the pride of motherhood, with a sorrow that was too deep for tears.

What was going through her mind we can only guess. Was this the time when she remembered that word spoken to her long ago in the temple when the aged Simeon had predicted that the day would come when the sword should pierce her heart also? Was this the time when she felt that stabbing pain in her soul, yet knew a peace beyond the pain because she believed that even this awful hour had its place in God's purpose?

We can only surmise what she felt as she saw her son hanging in death. But we know what he felt when he saw his mother standing loyally by his cross. Obviously by this time she was a widow, for there is no mention of Joseph anywhere in the story. And when the father of the family was gone, it became the duty of the eldest son to provide for his mother or, if he was unable to do it, to see that she was provided for.

It was this filial duty that our Lord now performed, commending his mother to the care and responsibility of John, the disciple whom he loved above all others. You may well ask why he did not give the responsibility of his mother to those to whom it belonged, his younger brothers and sisters. But the very fact that they were not there at the end should answer that question. Whether it was fear or shame or their old dislike of Jesus that kept them away, they had absented themselves from Calvary and so had forfeited their right and responsibility to another.

Now I do not think it unfair or unkind to say that Jesus had been a strange child and that Mary had not always found her motherhood easy. Way back when he was twelve he had begun to show unusual traits of independence. He had run away from his family without telling a soul. What may have occurred between that and his thirtieth birthday we cannot say. But then when Mary was probably already a widow, badly in need of financial help, with a home to maintain, mouths to feed, children to clothe, her eldest son whose duty it ought to have been to provide had left her. I dare say she had some consciousness that he had another work to do. I am certain that Jesus did not leave her without some financial provision. But it was hard sledding all the same. And the resentment of his younger brothers who had to take their place in the carpenter's shop at an early age had not made it any easier.

Nor did the growing picture of resentment and rejection help her position. At first, when Jesus had swept everything before him in a tide of popular acclaim, she had been glad to give him up and bask a little in his reflected glory. But as Jesus' support gradually fell away, as the opposition to him in Jerusalem gathered strength, as reports came back to her in Nazareth of the strange things that he was saying and even stranger things that he was doing, she found it harder and harder to accept the situation, until finally she resolved to bring Jesus back home to Nazareth. Probably he was fatigued, overworked. Probably he needed rest, good food, a mother's care.

And so she went one day with her family to ask Jesus to come back home, standing eagerly outside the door of the house where he was speaking. And then the incredible message came. Jesus would not see them. She was not his mother; they were not his brothers. He had a new family and no longer needed them.

No, being the mother of Jesus had not been easy. And now here at the cross the worst that she had feared had finally come to pass. And yet, there she is by the side of her dying son. She might have said, "He made his own bed; let him lie in it." She might have said, "He didn't need me then; let him get on without me now." She might have said, "Last year when I tried to get him to come home, he didn't know who his mother was; I don't know who my son is." She might have done as apparently her other children did, and gone home to hide herself for shame at having a criminal in the family. She might have—but she didn't.

Many waters cannot quench love, neither can the floods drown it. We may not believe that Mary is the queen of heaven. But we dare not forget that Mary is the superb example of the power of human loyalty and the strength of human love. Indeed, these two figures at the foot of the cross are unforgettable pictures of what our human relationships ought to be...John, the friend who stands by to the end, whose friendship is deeper than chance or change, whose loyalty lasts...Mary, the mother whose love will allow no misunderstanding, no imagined or real neglect, no false pride or shame keep her from the place where she belongs.

I know that many times our friendship is not like this, that it has a way of disappearing when things are hard. It is so easy to grow cynical about friendship when it can vanish so quickly. You see it here at the cross. The three intimate associates of Jesus in his early life were Peter, James, and John. And now in the hour of crisis Peter was gone, James was gone, but John was there, almost as if to show us what human friendship so often is not, and yet what it can be.

And I know also that many times our family life is not like this. Indeed, like most ministers, I have learned how twisted and bitter family life can become, how easily close intimacy can become blazing hatred. Well, you see this here at Calvary too. Jesus' brothers and sisters were not there. They were home crying in their pillows for the shame he had brought upon them, home nursing their resentment against that crucified fool to whom unfortunately they were related. But his mother was there, again almost as if to show us what family love so often is not, and yet what it can be.

But I turn from these two lesser figures to the central one, to the man upon the cross. For if in Mary and John we catch the meaning of human loyalty and human love, in Jesus we see the meaning of divine love and divine loyalty. And it is unforgettable.

I wonder if you realize how surprising our Lord's word is. What would you expect someone to say under these circumstances? "Look, John, this is no place for my mother. Take her home with you and get her away from this." That would be very human and understandable, a perfectly natural wish to spare her further suffering. "Mother, this isn't so bad as it seems. Dry your tears and remember that we shall meet again in a better world." That too would be perfectly natural, a desire to comfort and console.

But the surprising thing is that our Lord's first thought for his mother is neither for her protection or consolation, but for her sheer financial well-being and economic necessity. On the cross itself, bearing the sin of the world, about to stare down the bottomless abyss of divine desertion, Jesus Christ remembers first of all the physical and economic well-being of his mother.

I can think of no more dramatic illustration of a truth that we are always tending to forget. Indeed, it is a persistent heresy on the part of many Christian folk that if only you can extract a person's soul from the rest of the person, you can minister to it as a little entity all by itself. Well, Jesus Christ never thought that way, not even in the stress and pain of dying. He was always aware of the primary and essential wants of the whole person, the entire personality. And surely God's concern is no less.

It is a terrible thing when your religion is so elevated that it is above the ordinary needs of human life. Yet that is precisely the fate which has overtaken the religion of so many of us. Our religion is on a Sunday level, while we live on a Monday-through-Saturday level. So often I hear the complaint that Christianity is impractical and idealistic, with nothing to say to the ordinary needs and common problems of everyday living. But I also observe that those who make the complaint most often believe in a God so far away and so removed from this mortal scene that God nowhere touches the problems and needs of everyday living.

All that I can say is that if you worship a God to whom you would never think of turning with the routine concerns and ordinary affairs that make up nine-tenths of our lives, you are not worshiping the God and Father of our Lord Jesus Christ but some idol of your own design. So many of us are familiar with the God of the crisis, but we have never encountered the God of the commonplace. Our God is there to deal with birth, sickness, death, disaster. But we should never dream of disturbing God with matters of household finance, family relationships, job difficulties, problems in school. Our religion is just too elevated for real life.

Yet is it not true that we shall find God in the crisis only when we have effectively made his acquaintance in the commonplace? And is it not true that the God of the gospel wants to permeate all our living, no matter how commonplace, how trivial, with a sense of his presence? Whenever we are tempted to believe that there are aspects of our living too ordinary for God, too routine to be of concern to him, we can remember this third word from the cross. Whenever we are tempted to shove religion off into a compartment labeled "crisis," to limit its effectiveness to those rare moments of spiritual exaltation and mental elevation, we can remember this third word from the cross.

It is a precious insight into the heart of God. The trivial necessities, the commonplace routines, the ordinary sequence of life's events are just as important, just as much in need of his healing love and care as life's crises and its glories. For ours is a God whose concern is with all of our lives all of the time. To God, as he has made himself known in Christ, nothing is trivial, nothing unimportant.

And then this last word....God thinks of us before we think of him. The evangelist records no word from Mary on this occasion. She stands before the cross a silent figure only to discover that even in death Christ was more concerned with what he could give to her than what she could bring to him. And beyond that insight into the heart of God we cannot go. Do you know the prayer that says that God is always more ready to hear than we to pray? Well, here you see those words enacted in dramatic form. How often in our living and believing we vilify and slander the heart of God, pretending that he shows neither interest nor concern, claiming that he does nothing, shutting our eyes to the countless ways in which our prayers are answered—ways, to be sure, which we did not expect, but ways which surpass the things for which we asked.

God's concern for us always outruns and outreaches our concern for him. Here is the abiding meaning of this third word from the cross. And what a magnificent assurance for living it is! If our relationship with him were on a cash-and-carry basis, if we could count upon God's attention only in response to our attention, how impoverished and empty our lives would be. If God's favors to us were only the return of our favors to him, how little of God any of us would have in our living.

But that is not the case. God never forgets. God never grows indifferent. The initiative, the first word, is always God's. Do not blame God for being niggardly with his goodness. Rather blame yourself for being blind to the manifest signs of his goodness and tokens of his love which crowd upon your life from every side. For Jesus who on the cross could not forget his mother can and will never forget us, his brothers and sisters.

5

The Fourth Word

My God, my God,
why hast thou forsaken me?
Matthew 27:46, Mark 15:34

Can you stand on Calvary, listen to this fourth word from the cross, and not feel that it marks the end of mankind's one last slender hope? The man who for three years has preached trust in God, the burden of whose message for three years has been faith in the loving heart of a Father in heaven, is dying. And in his last moments on earth Jesus is apparently unable to practice what he has been preaching.

For all the world it looks as though at the decisive moment Jesus Christ's faith failed. And if that be true, then our last hope has vanished with these words. For if at the point of agony and suffering our blessed Lord himself was not able to keep his faith and his trust unbroken, what hope can there be for ours? If climbing Calvary was more than his faith could take, what must become of ours when we climb our lesser Calvaries?

And yet, though what I have said remains true in the realm of theory, I do not think that most of us really feel that way when we hear this fourth word from the cross. For whatever intellectual

29

disappointments and frustrations we should feel at having our deepest questions about life left unanswered are more than lost in our feeling of kinship with the man who could speak such words as these. Whether Jesus got his answer or not, here at least is someone who has shared the experience of my human situation down to its very bottom.

I admire and worship the man who in the agony of crucifixion says, "Father, forgive them; for they know not what they do." But I must worship and admire from a distance because I know that nothing in me is capable of that selfless reaction to suffering. But the man who in pain cries out, "My God, my God, why hast thou forsaken me?" is heart of my heart and mind of my mind. He has entered the darkest mystery of human life, the mystery of defeated goodness and victorious evil, the mystery of human lostness and abandonment. Standing by Jesus' cross, I recognize him as one who has shared the tragedy and uncertainty of human life to the last full measure.

But you may reply, "Does not that very fact only make the situation worse?" Yes, does not the fact that Jesus Christ, better than anyone else, knew what loneliness and desertion and despair are only deepen the tragedy? For if Jesus Christ knew them so well, why did he not show us the answer to them? Experiencing our human loneliness and perplexity so keenly, he should have been able to provide us with the solution for them. Life involves us, heaven knows, in enough situations when we ask *why*, never finding the answer. But to discover Jesus Christ sharing our place of darkness and uncertainty, unable to find an answer to his *why*, is almost the final tragedy.

It may draw us to him; it may make us more aware of our common humanity; it certainly heightens the pathos of these last hours on Calvary. But it leaves the permanent riddle of humanity unsolved. Over all our innocent suffering, all our undeserved pain, all our unmerited sorrow, Jesus Christ or no Jesus Christ, there is still written the unanswered question, "Why?"

And yet, you know, I rather think that the question, at least in the form in which our Lord asked it, contains its own answer. It is, of course, a quotation from the twenty-second Psalm. Every Jewish lad was brought up on the Psalms. They were a staple item in the diet of his education. Our Lord, therefore, would have been as familiar with the twenty-second Psalm as you and I are with the twenty-third. Was Jesus quoting from it here, even perhaps quoting the entire Psalm to himself as an act of prayer and devotion, though those standing by caught only this, its opening verse? Or was this cry from the cross no quotation at all, but something born from the anguish and desolation of his own heart at the moment?

Well, I do not pretend to have the answer. But whether a quotation or Jesus' own question, the important thing to see is that these words answer the very question that they ask, offer the only possible solution to the problem which they put. "*My* God, *my* God, why hast thou forsaken me?"

We need spend no time describing what our Lord felt when he spoke these words. Though to an infinitely smaller degree, we have all known the feeling. We have it whenever we feel that life has treated us harshly and unfairly, when we feel that we have been asked to shoulder burdens greater than we can bear, greater than we deserve to bear, whenever we feel that some situation of suffering, our own or that of someone we love, is totally and absolutely undeserved. Above all, it comes over us when we feel that in this place of pain God doesn't care, God offers no help, God has turned away and forgotten. That was what Jesus Christ felt at this moment. We know what he felt for we have felt it too and we have asked the same question.

But is it the same question? I have known many people who in difficult and hard situations have cried out, "Why? Why did this happen to me?" A husband loses his wife, a mother loses her son, a man loses his sight, a woman loses her hearing. And instinctively the question which comes to their lips is, "Why?" Why should life be so unfair? Why should the universe be so cold and unfeeling?

Why should fate be so bitter and cruel? So certain are we that the world must be rational, that life must operate in terms of justice as we understand it, that when something irrational or unjust happens to us we are determined to track down the reason for it, certain that there must be some reason, unwilling to admit to ourselves or anyone else that this world could be that crazy.

And I can see how such a person—and that would include many of us—seeing Jesus Christ hanging on his cross and hearing him speak this fourth word, would say, "See, even Jesus Christ himself was finally forced to ask why! And even Jesus Christ himself went out of this life without getting an answer! What can there be in the gospel for me?"

Ah, but they are misreading the story. Jesus Christ, hanging in death on his cross, did not ask why. At least he did not ask it in the way in which we do. He did not fling out his question to an impersonal and unfeeling universe. He did not question the rationality of life or the justice of fate. That is the first great difference between Jesus' question and ours. When we ask why, we address the question to life or fate or the universe, almost as though we believed life were some kind of calculating machine that should invariably ring up happiness for the good and misery for the bad. And when in our opinion the results get mixed up—the good get misery while the bad get happiness—then it is time to question the operation of the machine, time to ask why.

But if we ask why in that way, we never can get an answer. To question what happens to us on the basis that it never ought to happen to us is to ask a question better not asked, since it has no answer. Jesus Christ, hanging on his cross, did not ask why, addressing his question to fate, luck, or the rational structure of the universe. He put his question to God. And that begins to make it a different question.

What is so different about it, you ask? Have not many people in their distress and despair asked, "Why did God do this to me?" "Why does God send that to me?" "What have I done that God should treat me so?" What difference does it make whether they question their luck or question God? What difference does it make whether they complain about the rationale of the universe or complain about the logic of the divine purpose? Changing the terms of the question does not bring the answer any nearer, does it?

But we still have not got the question straight. Jesus Christ hanging on his cross did not say, "Why did God forsake me?" I grant you that that is our question. But it is the wrong question. And it is wrong because it indicates that in our thinking and believing God is really a third party, somewhere on the outside of our living. We talk about God, read about God, listen to sermons about God, even believe in God.

But we believe in God the way we believe in the Taj Mahal or the North Pole. He is something we have heard about, read about. We know God is there, all right. But God is something we have never seen or known for ourselves. There is no firsthand knowledge, no personal acquaintance, no heart-to-heart relationship. That's the kind of knowledge of God we have. And of course it is the kind that always goes to the wall. This is the kind of God who is so easily shattered by our troubles, the God that has always remained on the outside of our lives, a permanent stranger, one *about* whom we always speak but *with* whom we have never spoken.

I tell you, if that were the only God Jesus Christ had known, the first touch of the nails on his flesh would have made him an atheist. "Why does God do this to me?" is about as useful a question as asking what kind of tooth-paste the King of Siam uses. For in either instance, by the very way the question is phrased, we indicate that we are talking about someone so far away that any real knowledge about him is virtually impossible. Jesus Christ hanging on his cross did not question God as a third party, an outsider, a remote stranger, but *my* God. And because Jesus put his question that way, it contained its own answer.

"My God, why hast thou forsaken me?" is a very different question from "Why has God forsaken me?" Even there in that place of despair and anguish, our Lord did not speak about God of whom he had heard and in whom he had been led to believe. Even on Calvary, Jesus spoke with a God whom he personally knew and personally trusted...not God, but *my* God...not, "Why has he?" but, "Why have *you*?" Even though Jesus questioned God's ways, failed to grasp his purpose, was unable to fathom his activity, of this one thing he was certain, of this one thing he would not let go: this darkly mysterious God was still his Father. My God. Never once did Jesus permit the direst circumstances to make God a stranger or an enemy. Even in loneliness, lostness, and forsakenness, *my* God.

And here is the reason why this apparently darkest moment in the gospel is really one of the brightest, why this word of despair which we think contains no answer actually contains the only answer that will hold against all doubts and all questions. No one will deny that the life of any one of us will contain, if it has not done so already, many hard moments, many difficult problems, many strange events. They are the raw materials out of which our lives must be made, whether we like them or not.

Well, in the face of these things, there are only two answers that can finally satisfy. Either the whole panorama of life is one gigantic tale told by an idiot and the story of our lives has no more meaning than the scrawlings of a baby—either that, or *my* God—difficult to understand, hard to follow, with uncompromising demands, but always known, always trusted, always my God. It must be either one thing or the other.

If it be the first, then light your candle and go out into the dark alone as bravely as you can, knowing that sooner or later a breath of chill air will snuff out its flame forever. But if it be the second, remember that though life may sweep everything else away from you, so long as you can keep this elemental creed you can go in hope. My God. Not the God of the universe, not the God of the Bible, not the God of the minister, not the God of the philosophers or the theologians, not the God of my father, my mother, or my Sunday school teacher, but *my* God.

I cannot question fate. It is completely arbitrary and knows no law. Today it does one thing, tomorrow another. What can I say? I cannot question the God of the universe, that vast and unknowable being who spins the stars like tops and spreads out galaxies like blankets. He is too vast for my tiny mind to comprehend. How could I possibly think that such limitless intelligence heeded my queries?

But I can question my God, not because I have the right to answers, not because he owes me anything whatsoever, but because he is my God whom I know, whom I trust, whom I love. Whenever I question him, I know I shall always receive an answer which, though it may not at the time solve the superficial riddles posed by my intelligence, will always meet those deeper needs posed by my heart. Here is the only satisfying answer to life's intricate and troubling questions—to have faith to bring them to a God who is personally known, personally trusted, personally loved. God will make his own way plain.

6

The Fifth Word

I thirst.
John 19:28

Seven times Jesus spoke while he hung on his cross. But of the seven words he spoke, here is the only one that you or I could have said. Who of us, in the torment of crucifixion, would have called upon God, even to ask why did you forsake me? But what is expressed here is a need so human that any of us could have spoken it. This fifth word has nothing to do with religion, morality, or character, but entirely with sheer physical need. I am thirsty.

Who would not have been, hanging for three hours beneath a blazing eastern sun while his life's blood ebbed away? I am told that of all the needs of the human body, thirst is far and away the most agonizing. A person can endure hunger for a fairly long period of time. It is amazing how much physical pain the human body can take. But thirst is like a consuming fire. The most devastating, the most intense agony anyone can know is to feel the tongue thicken and the throat parch for lack of water. I thirst.

It ought not to surprise us, therefore, that sooner or later there should come from the lips of the Crucified this cry of human need.

The surprise comes only when you set this whole scene in the context of our Christian faith about Jesus Christ. If, as some hold, Jesus Christ was a man and only a man, albeit the finest and fairest flower of humanity, who on Calvary died a martyr's heroic yet tragic death, then, though his word is touching in its pathos, it does little more than remind us poignantly of the suffering which he endured before he died. If Jesus Christ was purely human and nothing more, then there would be little more to say about these words. What message would there be in these two words, which simply draw attention to the fact that crucifixion is a painful way to die?

But if Jesus Christ was and is what our Christian faith asserts— the Son of the living God, the translation into human personality of the divine mind and the divine heart—then even these two words glow with meaning and burn brightly with significance. Consider how far they take us into the inmost character of God. Doubtless you have discovered how many of the words of our language are symbolic, so that the selfsame word will suggest very different things to very different people. The word "gentleman," for example, will bring at least twenty different pictures to the minds of twenty people.

Well, what does that single yet all-important word "God" suggest to you? What picture does it call up to your mind? There would be some whose immediate vision would be of an old man with a long white beard sitting on a big throne with angels hovering around. There would be some who would see in their mind's eye one of those pictures of the Good Shepherd that used to adorn the covers of Sunday school leaflets. And there would be some who could get no clear picture at all, but only a vague impression of what somebody once called "an oblong blur."

But how many, I wonder, when they hear the word "God" would see a man nailed to a cross, murmuring with parched lips, "I thirst"? Yet that is exactly the picture of God presented to us in this scene. Each of these seven last words is a precious photograph of the mind and heart of God. But this one is a picture that requires considerable

study. I said earlier that this fifth word was one which had to do not
with religion, morality, or character, but with sheer physical need.
And that, of course, is true. But the fact that the gospel presents us
a picture of God in a position of purely physical need has everything
to do with religion. The fact that at the center of our faith you find
not the figure of a remote and awful deity, not some heroic
superman, not some discarnate spirit who lives beyond human
pain, but one divine enough to forgive and human enough to be
thirsty—that fact makes our Christian faith unique, different from
all the religions of the world.

And if I do nothing else with it, I hope I can make this picture of
God vivid and real. A few years ago there appeared a very
stimulating book entitled, *Is Your God Too Small?* I recommend it
highly for in it the author, Dr. Phillips, presents a keen analysis of
the ways in which you and I commonly limit the mind of God,
narrow its scope, diminish its power so that we go through life with
only a fraction of what we might have if we pushed out the
boundaries of our understanding and faith.

But at the same time I think that the reverse question might be
asked of many of us. I ask it now in all seriousness, looking straight
at him who said, "I thirst." Is your God too big? A ridiculous
question, you say. How can you possibly have too big an idea of
God when eternity is not enough to contain him? How can God be
too big when, if you think yourself to the outermost bounds of
infinite space, you have only touched the hem of his garment? Well,
all that is true. But it is still possible to have a God who is too big
(and many of us have him), too big for the intimate and personal
needs of individual lives.

Would you not agree that this is what has happened to too many
of us? It is not that we do not believe in God; of course we do! But
between that belief and the heartaches, pains, problems, and
questions of life there is such a wide gulf. A problem has to be a big
one before we let God in on it. When there is a death in the family,
or when we must endure some terrible catastrophe, when there are

wars and rumors of wars, then we think that our problem has reached sufficiently large proportions to be of interest to God, and we want him.

But when you come right down to us, moments of that sort are relatively rare. And between them, life is filled with countless petty details, small questions, minor aches and pains which never see the healing light of God's presence. I admit that in part this is the result of our strange idea that we are competent for these things and need no help, often, indeed, resenting it when it is offered. But I am also certain that in no small measure it is the result of our idea that God is too big, too far away, to be interested or to care.

But that is not the case. Strike from your mind those pictures of God as a venerable old man sitting on a distant throne, peering down occasionally with curiosity at the affairs of the world below. That is not the God of the gospel, but a pathetic idol, the worship of which will cut you off from the peace and joy, courage and hope that you need and can have.

Here is the God of the gospel, a poor, pathetic dying man who pleads for a little water to moisten his cracked and burning lips. You may call it an incredible picture, a daring picture, a silly picture, if you like. You may call it anything you please. But you can never stand at the cross, hear this fifth word, and say that the God of the gospel is impervious to human suffering, unconcerned with human pain, too big to be bothered with human need. We may go through life thinking of God as a blind and unpitying force in the sky. But here at the cross we are brought up short to learn that it is not so. In the lovely lines of William Blake,

> Till our grief is fled and gone,
> He doth sit by us and moan.

That's the God of the gospel, caring for every human need because he has shared every human need, even the simplest and most elemental of all. *I thirst.*

But there is a second feature to the God of the gospel that comes out in this fifth word from the cross. I think of the sheer honesty of this scene as compared with so many of the shams and pretensions about life in which we so commonly indulge ourselves. As a minister, I spend more time with sufferers than most, whether their pain be physical or those deeper afflictions of mind and spirit. And out of that experience I am often led to consider the ways in which we try to meet these situations of suffering and pain.

Sometimes we try the "silver-lining-in-the-cloud" tack and try to persuade ourselves and our friends that things are not really so bad as they seem. You know the kind of Job's comforter who is always telling you how much worse things might have been than they are. Sometimes we vary our routine by trying to persuade others how much better they are than they think. Here is one of the commonest attitudes toward trouble. We go to all kinds of lengths, sometimes fanciful, sometimes ingenious, sometimes downright deceitful, to avoid facing the ugly fact for what it is. We minimize suffering, anesthetize pain, explain away sin, decorate death till it is all but unrecognizable. This is all the religion that many people know, the ability to pretend their way out of trouble. Cheer up, it's not so bad as it might have been!

Or there are those whose way of meeting life's hardships is that of the stoic. They bite their lips, grit their teeth, tense their bodies, and plunge ahead. There must be no tears, no sighing, no stopping to ask questions, no show of weakness. There are those who think that the highest form of religion is never to let anyone know what you feel, never let anyone suspect that you have the slightest emotion, even in the most terrible moments of life.

If under extreme pressures they can maintain their dogged and sullen self-control, they think they have accomplished a mighty wonder. And though they may never have thought the matter through, their attitude clearly reveals that they think suffering and pain are simply things to be endured. Their hero is the one who like a dumb animal bears whatever burdens life presents.

But do you see anything like that on the cross? Jesus Christ is in pain. But he does not pretend. There is about Calvary a rugged honesty that cannot fail to impress, whatever may be your religious convictions. Here is no pretending that things are not so bad as they seem. Here is no silly effort to find the silver lining in the cloud. Here is no deluded attempt to dismiss pain as imaginary or sorrow as unimportant. Here are human sin and human suffering in all of their savage reality. *I thirst.*

And by the same token, here are no mock heroics, no false bravado. Hanging on his cross, the son of God does not hold back. True, Jesus restrains his own sense of suffering until he has thought of others, the tormentors, the companion in death, his mother. But then, when the awareness of his own agony is overwhelming, he allows no false pride to hold it back, no sense of shame to keep it in. *I thirst.* Frankly, unashamedly, honestly, I thirst.

I suppose that really it does not take us very far with this terrible problem of our humanity, the problem of sin and pain and suffering. But I wonder whether it does not take us a vast deal farther than we sometimes realize. Come right down to the bedrock of the gospel and what do you find? A God who says, "Cheer up, it's not so bad as you think"? A God who bids us keep a stiff upper lip since it will soon be over? No, you find a God who sharing the pain of our pain and the suffering of our suffering, cries, "I thirst."

Here at this old rugged cross are no sentimental pretenses, no mock heroics, no effort to make us angels or superhuman, but honest facing of the full facts of human existence in all of their grim reality. And with that I can begin and of that I can be certain. A God who pooh-poohed the suffering of life would not interest me. A God who bid me be a hero when I am a coward could not help me. But a God who has honestly faced and felt the same suffering I can follow. I do not know where it will come out. But at least I have a guide I can trust, since he has been where I must go.

And is not just this the power of the Christian faith? It presents us in Jesus Christ with a God not too big to care and not too far away to know. The only God who can meet our need is the God who has honestly known our need. If the New Testament presented me with a God who wrote prescriptions for human conduct and human need from the safe haven of his heaven where an occasionally peevish angel was his only problem, I should not be a preacher nor, I dare say, would you be a Christian. But when it pictures a God who offers no prescriptions, no panaceas, but simply goes the way I must go and gives the simple command to take up my cross and follow, my soul starts up in eager recognition. This God who shares my need can meet my need.

For I too thirst. George Meredith has a poem which contains the lines,

> Ah, what a dusty answer gets the soul
> When hot for certainties in this our life.

We thirst for certainty. We thirst for assurance. We thirst for meaning and significance. We thirst for peace and contentment. Our hearts are hot and dry and sometimes grow so parched we think we can no longer stand the pain. Here at the cross are no answers, no easy speeches, no quick solutions. But here is one who has opened the way to the waters of healing.

7

The Sixth Word

It is finished!
　　John 19:30

. . and what was finished?

The meaning of this sixth word from the cross is rather uncertain if we look no further than the word itself. Just these three words, taken by themselves, could constitute a very pathetic yet very human cry of weakness and defeat. It is finished. It is all over with now—the suffering, the pain, the scorn. Death will soon draw its merciful curtain across the scene. There are no more burdens to be borne. There is no more pain to be suffered, no more torment to be endured. The powers of death have done their worst. It is finished.

Yes, and more than life itself is finished. Finished are the dreams and hopes with which he had once enthralled the multitude. Finished is the teaching which had once rung with such authority. Finished is the mad career that just a few days earlier had drawn excited hosannas from hundreds of hearts. Finished is that kingdom the coming of which he had proclaimed so confidently. To what other conclusion can you come when a man who claimed to be a king hangs there nailed like a bat to a barn door? At least Jesus had the wit to see it himself, the courage to admit the shattering of his illusions before he died. It is finished.

It would be perfectly possible on the basis of these three words to conclude that this was the way in which our Lord took his leave of life, gladly accepting the end, when it came, as a merciful release, meekly bowing his head to breathe his last. And much as you could have wished the end to be something else, what could you say? What could you say indeed but that at the last, as with all of us, the world proved too much for Jesus too? It is finished.

But if you look a little beyond these three words, you will see that such was not the case at all. For one thing, only St. John records this next-to-the-last word, "It is finished." The other three evangelists do not tell us what Jesus said at this point in the story. But all three of them record the fact that just before he died, he cried with "a loud voice." And by the words that they use, they indicate clearly what they mean.

For this "loud voice" is exactly the phrase which is used in Greek to indicate a victor's shout, a triumphant cry, such as might rise from the throat of a runner who was first to cross the finish line in a race, such as might escape from the lips of a tired but happy wrestler who had won a difficult match. St. John apparently understood the words which the other three had heard only as a victor's shout. But putting the two accounts together makes it clear that these words were not whispered weakly as a last sad farewell to life but shouted triumphantly as the victor crossed the goal.

But more than that, there is the word itself which came from Jesus' lips. In Greek it is not, as in English, three words which might mean one of several things, but a single word which can mean one thing and one thing only. *Tetelestai!* Finished! Accomplished! Achieved! Here is no weak admission that, thank God, it's all over with now. Here is the triumphant assertion that the job which was to be done has been completed. The mission that was assigned has been accomplished. In spite of incredible difficulties, in spite of almost insurmountable barriers, he has done it. Now let them say what they will, do what they may. They can neither injure nor destroy what he has completed. The word which Jesus chose is rich with purpose and the tense he used indicates the completion of that purpose. It is finished. With every flag proudly waving, with every banner still flying defiantly, the ship has been brought safely to port.

Perhaps you have heard the alto aria, "It is finished," in Bach's *Passion According to St. John*. It begins with a setting of the words which is almost a sob. You can hear the sorrow of humanity in it. But Bach was too good a theologian, too keen a Christian, to let it stop there. Immediately the trumpets sound the note of victory, and the solo continues: "The Lion of Judah has conquered!" That's the only way in which these words are rightly understood. Even while the sobbing sounds, the trumpets of victory echo over it. The Lion of Judah has conquered. It is finished!

But now, exactly what was finished? Our original question still stands, even though we now know the manner in which Jesus spoke these words. What is finished? His life, to be sure. But what had Jesus accomplished, what had he completed with the ending of his life? What was this goal the achievement of which gave our Lord such a conviction of victory as he died, transforming death into a triumph?

To be sure, there are many ways in which we could answer that question. To be surer still, there are many answers to that question which lie beyond the poor power of our minds to grasp and understand. But no one who studies the life of our Lord even casually can fail to perceive that Jesus was a man with a mission. Even as a boy of twelve he was conscious that he ought to be about his Father's business. And in the maturer years of his ministry, his Father's business was the motive for every word that Jesus spoke and every deed that he did.

It was his Father's business that took Jesus through Galilee preaching the kingdom of God and his righteousness. It was his Father's business that moved Jesus with compassion when he saw the multitude. It was his Father's business that led Jesus to heal the sick and forgive the sinner. It was his Father's business that brought Jesus willingly to Pilate's judgment hall. It was his Father's business that made Jesus stumble up Calvary with the heavy cross. It was his Father's business that nailed Jesus to that tree. And now it was his Father's business which Jesus had completed with the victorious cry, "It is finished."

And what was his Father's business? We used to say that it was the saving work of Jesus Christ in both life and death to bring humanity back to God. I certainly should not wish to dispute the truth of that statement. But I do not think it contains the deepest truth about our Lord. More profoundly and deeply still, it was Jesus' business to bring God back to humanity.

An extreme statement in view of the fact that God had never left us? True. But what happened all through Jesus' life, climaxed by his death on the cross, was not just that our Lord led us back from the wasteland of our living to the old familiar place where God had been waiting all along. In Jesus Christ, God himself came right into the wasteland of our living, there to live, there to die. If it was our sin that kept us from finding God, very well, he would come right into the midst of our sin and dare its consequences. If it was our pride that kept us from finding God, very well, he would come right into the midst of our pride and take its penalty. And this cry marks the last possible point he could reach in so dangerous a venture. For not even love can go further than dying.

I say it was a dangerous venture. To come with the sinful and yet be free from sin, to be with the doubting and yet not give way to doubt, to be with the hateful and yet never fall victim to hate's control—that sounds like a difficult, if not impossible, task. But that was the task Jesus had now finished. In terms of human personality he had drawn the likeness of God for humanity without once blurring the lines or distorting the picture.

Anyone can talk about God in the quiet of a church or the calm of a study hall, speculating as to God's nature, theorizing about

God's character. But our Lord lived the life of God in all the heat and dirt, the blood and tears of our human situation without one betrayal of his mission, one failure in his task. One word of doubt, one answer of hatred, one show of weakness, one surrender to some lesser goal, and Jesus would have been a failure, presenting a false god to the human mind and heart.

But that had not happened, not even in the pain and agony and weariness of these last three hours. Finished! In Jesus Christ, God has found us. In Jesus Christ, we have found God. What matters that it cost Jesus his life? It was worth it to be able to show us a finished sketch, in lines which we can not possibly misread, of the mind and heart of God.

And I must say that I wish something more of this note could be found in our understanding of the cross. So much of it is so weakly sentimental, the shedding of pious tears for the poor savior and what he suffered there. We should save our tears for ourselves. Calvary is no wailing wall. It is history's most terrifying battleground. The powers of hell, of death and sin there unleash against Jesus the whole arsenal of their weapons, those same weapons with which they have defeated us time and again. But they cannot defeat him. They cannot capture Jesus as they have captured us. Alone he stands against them and drives them beaten from the field. Look up at the cross; brush away the tears. Sing, my tongue, the glorious battle! Praise, my heart the wondrous Victor! The Lord is reigning from the tree! *It is finished.*

But now just a postscript, as it were. In the deepest sense of the word, it is finished. But in a lesser, though not unimportant sense, it is not finished. And that is why we have Good Fridays. For though the sketch has been drawn, the picture painted, completely and finally, the battle won once and for all, in all the turmoil and confusion of our living it is so easy to forget, to wonder, to lose the vision and its assurance.

We need to see not just once but often the love of God hanging triumphantly on a cross. With all of our doubts and fears, we need to be assured once again that God so loves the world. We need some tangible token that all this is not somebody's hopeful guess, some empty preachment, but burning reality. That is why time and again we gather to hear the old, old story. That is why we take bread and break it, lift the cup and drink it. This is my body broken for you. This is my blood of the New Testament shed for you.

The God who found us in Jesus Christ will never leave us. The love that grasped us at Calvary will never let us go. The victory of the cross is true today, tomorrow, always. *It is finished!*

8

The Seventh Word

*Father, into thy hands
I commend my spirit.*
  Luke 23:46

There is not one of the seven last words of our Lord which contains stranger contrasts than this, the seventh and the last. Here in this final word from the cross there is pathos and there is power. There are tears, but there is triumph. And if we really are to have a full picture of this last moment in the earthly life of our Lord, we must see them both.

For if we see the pathos without the power, the tears without the triumph, the death of Jesus Christ becomes nothing but history's great tragedy, a sad song that must be played throughout in a minor key. And if we see the power without the pathos, the triumph without the tears, the death of Jesus Christ becomes nothing but a piece of divine play-acting, completely unrelated to the suffering and sorrow of our human lives. It is only when we see both that we understand how the death of Jesus Christ can be what the Christian faith has always asserted—an event in which God shared the misery of our human existence to the full and by his very sharing of it redeemed it into glory.

Let me begin, therefore, by calling your attention to something which at first sight may not seem to be very important. This last sentence that our Lord spoke is, with the exception of a single word, another quotation from the Psalms. The fifth verse of the Thirty-first Psalm reads, "Into thy hands I commend my spirit." To that quotation Jesus added the single word, "Father."

In itself there would be nothing unusual about such a quotation. For the Psalms were both the hymnal and the prayer book of Hebrew religion. There was hardly any lad in Palestine who had not committed them to memory as part of his religious education. In times of great exaltation or of deep distress, various words of the psalter would naturally come to mind as the finest expression of the heart's deepest feelings. Once before this, you will recall, our Lord had quoted from another psalm when he cried, "My God, my God why hast thou forsaken me?" It need occasion no surprise, therefore, that once again and for the last time Jesus fell back upon the Psalms to express what was in his heart.

But there is something more about this last word from the cross. Do you know what little Hebrew children were taught to say by their mothers before they closed their eyes at night, much as you and I were taught "Now I lay me down to sleep"? *Into thy hands I commend my spirit.* That very Friday night in countless homes in Palestine when the mothers had tucked their little ones in their beds and blown out the lights, they would hold their hands and listen while little lips formed this prayer. *Into thy hands I commend my spirit.*

Thirty years before in such a home in Nazareth time after time Mary had kissed her son good night and then listened while he said his evening prayer. *Into thy hands I commend my spirit.* And now that same son, grown to manhood, climaxing his ministry on a cross, can find no better way to take farewell of life than that which he had learned at his mother's knee. *Father, into thy hands I commend my spirit.*

I find something infinitely moving and especially instructive in that picture. It brings the cross down from those theological heights where we so often isolate it to our level of understanding. In his final moment of suffering Jesus Christ spoke not some lofty discovery of the mature religious mind, some bit of esoteric wisdom to be shared only by a few, but a childhood prayer, very likely the first prayer that he had ever learned, one that had stayed with him through the years and now at the end was still able to nourish his soul.

The shadows have lengthened and the evening has come. The busy world is hushed, the fever of life is over, and his work is done. The wheel has turned full circle. Did Jesus in those last moments see once again the old familiar home in Nazareth, the face of his mother bending over him, as like a tired child he rested his weary head? *Father, into thy hands I commend my spirit.*

I said that there was something instructive here too. Let me call your attention to it. The religious forms and experiences of our adult lives are certainly important, as they deepen, strengthen, and confirm the faith that we have learned at home, in church, in Sunday school. But nothing human is of greater consequence for our souls than the first religious impressions of childhood. These we almost never lose. Time may change their shape, alter their form, deepen their meaning. But time will never erase them. More than anything else they will be the things to which we return when skies are dark and going is hard. The very first things we teach our children about God are the things they will remember the longest. You may think that their little minds do not grasp or understand. You may wonder why it is necessary to bother with religious training at all when its content is so much greater than they can comprehend. Here is the answer. Even when everything else disappears, this remains. Jesus Christ's last word from his cross was the little prayer he had learned at his mother's knee. *Father, into thy hands I commend my spirit.*

We have spoken of the pathos. We have seen the tears. Now for the power and the triumph, for they are certainly here too. And it would be a pity indeed if the tears and the pathos made them obscure to our minds. In one sense these words are a prayer. But in another sense, like every good prayer, they are a creed. They are

Jesus Christ's final conviction about life and its meaning, hammered out in the agony of a cross. This last word is not simply a farewell to mortality. The last word is Jesus' last word on what life is and what life means.

And that last word, that creed, that final assertion can all be summed up in this. These our lives are held gently but firmly in the strong grasp of one who is not only intelligence but love. I find this last word from the cross the most impressive thing that Jesus Christ ever said. To be sure, this was not the first time that he had said it, had declared that this was his Father's world. The Sermon on the Mount, for example, echoes with that glad assertion. But it is one thing to say it where lilies wave and crowds gather, where the sky is blue and the sunlight sparkles. It is one thing to say in such a setting with a heart full of joy that God is love and that his hand is upon all we do or experience. You will forgive me, but I think that I could have said the same thing then and there.

But this is another mount. Here are no lilies, but thorns. The crowds have thronged not to listen, but to mock. The sun has been swallowed up in darkness and the sky is heavy. The heart is no longer full of joy, but bursting with sorrow. And yet this cross is a sermon on the mount more telling than that which he had preached before. For in this sermon Jesus preaches not with words but with his life. And yet the text remains unchanged! *Father...thy hands. . . .*

And that makes this sermon on the mount unforgettable. For here was no evidence of a Father—the sun grown dark with mystery; the body aching, bleeding, and sore; the cause deserted even by those who had professed it. Does this look to you like the handwork of a Father or the cruel joke of a fiend? And here certainly was no sign of the hand of God. Where would you trace it on that bleak and desolate hill crowned with three crosses? Where would you find it in that grim and murderous scene? It was not there, you say; and if Jesus Christ could find it, he was simply making grandiose statements that were not true.

But you are wrong! You know Jesus Christ well enough to know that he never made a statement of which he was not himself convinced. You know Jesus Christ well enough to know that bluff and bravado were not in him. If in the darkness and death of Calvary Jesus Christ was still convinced that his life was held in the grasp of an omnipotent hand, he said it because he believed it. He spoke it because he knew it.

For what are these hands of God that hold us? We seem to think that God keeps his hand behind his back, so to speak, never once interfering in the course of our lives or the direction of this world unless we happen to decide that he should. Then, in response to our demand we would like to see the heavens open and God's hand reach down to pick us up out of the dark valley and set us down once again in green pastures. After that, of course, we would like nothing better than for God to withdraw his hand and let us alone until we think we need him again.

I doubt that our Lord ever thought that way about the hand of God. He never thought of God as a big policeman who came running whenever we blew the whistle. And certainly neither the Bible nor our Christian faith sees God this way. The hand of God is not the strong arm of intervention which strikes out in massive retaliation against wrongdoers. No, the picture is quite another one.

In the darkness, confusion, mystery of our lives, the hand of God is something extended for us to grasp, for us to hold. Sometimes the path is rough. Sometimes the water is cold and deep. We may wonder why it should be that way. But it is that way and there is no better answer. Yet no matter how rough and dark the path, no matter how chill and deep the stream, there by your side, if you will reach out to grasp it, is the hand of Almighty Love. And if there is anything in life and death of which you may be sure, it is this. That hand is always there and will always be there.

You may not know where you are going. You may not know how you will get there. But this you can always know: the hand of God is stretched out to you in all of his strength. And once you grasp it,

God will never let you go—no, not even when you must enter that darkest valley and cross that coldest stream. Even then you can walk without fear, in full confidence that that same hand that has led you all the way will lead you safely across and up into those eternal hills that shine in their glory on the other side.

What then was Jesus Christ's final creed, his last conviction about human existence? Although for reasons which pass our understanding our lives contain materials that are rough and raw, the only person who needs to be without the strong hand of God is the person who chooses to be. For if we put out our hand in faith, we shall always find God's hand grasping ours in love. Like little children afraid to climb the stairs in the dark unless their father take them by the hand, so we cannot find our way unless our Father grasps us by the hand. But once we feel that powerful hand supporting us, we can go on and not be afraid. We can run and not be weary. We can walk and not faint.

The last word from the cross is no dying man's philosophy of life, no mere echo of a childhood prayer. It is the secret of victorious living, to be renewed every day that we live. Do we face problems that we cannot even begin to solve? *Into thy hands.* Do we experience sorrow we are sure we cannot bear? *Into thy hands.* Do we face temptations stronger than we can endure? *Into thy hands.* Is life with its many complications too much for us? *Into thy hands.* Are we staring across the great sea of eternity wondering what lies on the other shore, wondering if there is another shore? *Into thy hands.*

There is just nothing in life or in death, not even a cross, for which this word of final confidence is not the answer. You cannot explain your hardships. You cannot find the reason for your troubles. You will never in this world be able to live free from them. But put your hand in the hand of God and you will always find the way through.

This is not *my* word to you, though my little experience would tend to confirm it. This is the word of Jesus who first learned his faith at his mother's knee, who proclaimed it gladly to the thronging people, who spoke it tenderly to hearts that were sore and perplexed, who tested it in the harsh experience of crucifixion, who used it to shatter the barriers of darkness, sin, and death and let in the unquenchable light of life and love.

It is the word of Jesus Christ our Lord, guaranteed with his life's blood. For see, the hand that is stretched out to you in the darkness still bears the marks of the nails!

. . . and that is why we call this Friday good!

9

Prayer

Almighty God, we beseech thee graciously to behold this thy family, for which our Lord Jesus Christ was contented to be betrayed and given up into the hands of wicked men, and to suffer death upon the cross; who now liveth and reigneth with thee and the Holy Ghost ever, one God, world without end. Amen.

Part II

Good Friday 1968 Sermons
The Seven Last Words

These sermons were preached at the North Reformed Church in Newark, New Jersey, on Good Friday, 1968, following the assassination of Martin Luther King, Jr.

10

Introduction-1968

*For God so loved the world, that he gave his only
begotten Son, that whosoever believeth in him should
not perish, but have everlasting life.*
    John 3:16

This vigil by the cross should begin with a kind of open confession.
The Seven Last Words have long been the traditional texts for
Good Friday, and I have used them many times in the course of my
ministry. Some four years ago, in fact, one series of such meditations
eventually found its way into print and became a little devotional
book. Because my thoughts on these words have achieved that kind
of permanence, I had pretty well set them aside as things about
which I could have little left to say.

When, therefore, I was asked to conduct a three-hour service on
Good Friday, 1968, I assumed that the Seven Last Words would not
be the basis of what I had to say. I tried to work out several series
of addresses using other plans of organization. My thinking and
planning were still not certain when in early April of that year, like
everyone else, I was caught up in that amazing sequence of events
that culminated in the assassination of Martin Luther King. Out of
the emotional and spiritual experience of those days, watching the

television and reading the papers, walking the streets of my city a few nights in the hope that in that small way I could contribute to its peace and order, talking with friends and parishioners, joining the 25,000 persons who walked through the Newark slums on Palm Sunday, I found that the Seven Last Words began to speak out again.

Some years ago when I had written on the Seven Last Words (to another congregation), I wrote in very personal terms about their meaning for the understanding and strengthening of our own personal lives. And I believe that all that was valid and still is valid. But then in the assassination and all of the uprisings and tensions which followed it, the words, "Father, forgive them, for they know not what they do," began singing in my brain. And I found myself asking more and more, if this word is saying something to me in this situation, how about the others? Could I take a new look at all of them, looking at them now not from the angle of the penitent at the foot of the cross, but from the angle of the anguished and driven and strife-torn society? Could the last words of Christ also speak to that?

And as if in answer to my own question there came that most familiar of all gospel texts, John 3:16. God so loved the world—the world, the broken, fighting, ugly, unhappy world—that he gave his Son—because he wanted his world to have life and not death. If that be true, then why should the cross not speak to the urban crisis? If that be true, then does not this world which God loved and keeps on loving so much need to hear what the cross wants to say to it?

I suppose that a part of our problem lies in the fact that familiar as the words of John's gospel are to all of us, we have never thought them through. I don't honestly suppose that I had. As soon as we hear this great assertion, we immediately want to personalize it, to reach out and substitute *me* for the *world*, so that even while we hear the gospel saying, "God so loved the world," we are in reality thinking, "God so loved *me*."

Now I do not want entirely to scold this habit of ours. We have to personalize in order to grasp things. The trouble is that having made the personalization, we stop. God so loved me…and other people like me…who belong to the same church that I do…or now that we live in the ecumenical age, to other churches… But stop that; it's a terrible travesty. *God so loved the world.* Yes, that takes you in, friend, but it takes in a mighty lot else. It takes in the rioter and the militant; it takes in the white racist; it takes in Dr. King and it takes in his murderer. The cross is not our private possession. It was erected in the world for the world, to draw all unto God.

So that *all* might live—that is what God wants—that *all* might live. Right now they are dying, not just shot in the streets or having heart attacks in bed. They're dying inside; they are not experiencing the abundant life of real humanity. All people are not experiencing it, the person in the suburbs, the person in the ghetto. It's a sick society that is dying. O, it's coming alive to all kinds of things, to all kinds of panic and fear, to all kinds of smugness and self-righteousness, to all kinds of treachery, indifference, and deceit. "We who seven years ago talked of honor and of truth, shriek with pleasure when we show the weasel's fang, the weasel's tooth."

But it's a society, it's a world which is dying to all things that matter, to all the things that make for righteousness and for peace. And over such a world on Good Friday that cross of Jesus Christ stands again. And from that cross on such a Good Friday those seven last words are spoken again. Can it be that these seven words which have said so much to so many people in so many different situations throughout the centuries have nothing whatever to say to us in our situation on Good Friday in the America of the urban crisis?

I think they have much to say and my task today is to help them say it, to bring very different aspects and features of our human existence to the foot of the cross and let the Savior speak to them, to bring our particular world to the foot of the cross, and let it hear the message of life from this place of death.

While doing this, I am fully conscious that in all probability I shall not be speaking so much to that world as I am to the church. That is all right, because what other business does the church really have but to bring to the world the news that God so loves it that God wants it to live and has given his Son to make it live? For in some way or other that news has got lost in the ecclesiastical shuffle. We who should have seen it more clearly because we have experienced it most deeply have gone stale, become tired and weary. The fact is that the news for the most part is being taken to the world by other people, yes, even the news that we were entrusted to take.

Now I am not jealous of those other people, nor do I begrudge them what they are doing because I believe that the news is so important that God is going to see that it gets taken to the world without us. But I am jealous for us, the people of God, because by our refusal to do our job we are losing so much of our own integrity, yes, sacrificing so much of our own joy and peace. We are not living, not in any sense of abundance, because we seem to have lost our purpose. We're not quite sure any longer why the church is here or what it ought to be doing.

So I hope that these meditations may not only remind us of what it is that the cross says to the world, but that they may also help to recreate us and restore us to a real understanding of what it means to be the church in the world that God loves. Perhaps the seven times our Lord speaks may help us better understand the pattern of the church's life, may help us see why it is true that in so many aspects of our existence as the people of God we have been worrying about all the wrong things, so busy with them in fact, that the needful things seem to have eluded us and been forgotten.

Here we are, therefore, people out of the urban crisis, church people, God's people, but perplexed, unhappy, uncertain, frightened. It is our hour of agony as perhaps no other Good Friday in memory has ever been. There have been other agonizing Good Fridays before, in times of war or depression. But then the enemy was always someone over there whom we could see and with whom we could fight. Now the agony is that we are beginning to realize that the enemy is ourselves—all of us. There is just nowhere else to put the blame. And we do not really know how to cope with that discovery.

So in this time of agony, come with me to the foot of the cross and let us listen together as he speaks to us out of his hour of agony. But do not come to a martyr's death or to a religious theory. Come to the sign which says clearly and strongly, *God so loved the world that he gave his only begotten Son that whoso believeth in him should not perish but have everlasting life.*

11

The First Word-1968

Father, forgive them;
for they know not what they do.
   Luke 23:34

But once the magic of these words has begun to lose its spell and it is possible to think about the whole situation rationally and clearly, you will want to say, "Lovely as it is, this phrase is a piece of sheer sentimentality. For the fact is that they knew perfectly well what they were doing." And in light of the actual situation, it is hard to deny that, isn't it? We may perhaps excuse the soldiers themselves, the actual executants of the order for crucifixion. All they knew was that it was a soldier's duty to obey; any thought about the possible consequences or implications of their actions was for someone higher up to worry about, not for them.

And we should agree. What we are really dealing with here in the Good Friday story is a couple of establishments, one religious and the other political. And it is impossible to believe for a single moment that they did not know what they were doing. A young man who had become extremely offensive to the religious establishment, so offensive that his very existence seemed to pose a serious threat to it, had to be put out of the way. While it was true that the political establishment did not at the moment regard him with quite the same gravity, still there were enough possible risks involved in letting him live that Pilate was willing, after a show of reluctance, to let Caiaphas have his way. They didn't know what they were doing? Don't be silly. They knew perfectly well what they were doing. It was an artful and skillfully contrived plan that they had followed to make this cross possible.

And I make bold to point out that in our society today our opinion of things has not really changed very much. God knows that our establishments have been subject to all kinds of disorders in these recent months and years. And while here and there voices have been raised on behalf of forgiveness and understanding, the settled attitude and policy has been that there can be no talk of such things because here we are dealing with people who knew perfectly well what they were doing. Law and order have been violated by persons who had every intention of violating them.

When people stand on a street corner and cry, "Burn, baby, burn," or pass out recipes for making molotov cocktails, what do you mean they don't know what they are doing? Stop talking nonsense! It is too late for talking anyway. We have to act. We have to stop that kind of thing and stop it forcefully before it stops us. We are not interested in sociological or economic or even psychological explanations for the urban crisis, for our civil disorders. We are interested only in seeing that they be put down. And we are not in the slightest impressed by the sentimental claim that those who engage in them do not know what they are doing.

So for many of us the cross of Jesus Christ hangs on Good Friday over the burned-out sections of our cities as a meaningless symbol. Yes, privately we may go to it and have some personal moments rich in blessing. We are sure that God understands that we did not know what we were doing when we sinned, sure that God will forgive us our folly. But let us attempt to translate this first word from the cross into any kind of larger terms and immediately the forgiveness which we crave for ourselves becomes foolish sentimentality which no one would even dare apply to society.

But I am not sure that we can dismiss Jesus as a sentimentalist at this point. Certainly he was a sentimentalist at no other point in his life. Yes, it was true that those who had brought him to this place knew perfectly well what they were doing. Or did they? They had set out to rid themselves of a threat. But were they at all aware of the larger implications of their immediate purpose? Is anyone aware of the larger implications of the immediate purpose?

Well, this much can be said: Jesus Christ our Lord spent his life, yes, spent his death, trying to make us aware of them. For the immediate purpose of any group is to establish itself or, if it be established, to maintain itself. The immediate purpose of any group is to rid itself of threats, to destroy those who would destroy it. And the life-long message of Jesus Christ was simply this. The quest for dominance, the desire for control, the passion for ownership, these are destructive patterns of life which can only involve final ruin.

It was impossible for them to see it on Good Friday, but that Temple establishment was not destroying Jesus. It was destroying itself by its refusal to listen and to serve. It was even more impossible to see it that Good Friday, but the Roman Empire was not getting rid of Jesus; it was paving the way for its own destruction by its cowardly rejection of justice. They knew what they were doing and they did not know what they were doing.

Nor do we in our insistence upon violent and unyielding confrontations in our society. By setting class against class or race against race, by being quietly indifferent so long as our comfortable position is maintained, we do not know what we are doing. What we are doing is setting ourselves against the very way in which our Lord believed God has ordered this world. And the results of such violation of God's basic ordering of this world can only be catastrophic. "Jerusalem, Jerusalem, if only you had known the things that make for peace. But because you did not, not one stone shall be left standing upon another." The historian of the future will easily be able to point out where the empire began to crack, where the establishment made its fatal misstep. But by that time the empire will have gone and the establishment will have vanished because in all of their proud activity, they did not really know what they were doing.

And this is why this first word from the cross is such a mighty one. For against this tidal wave of ignorant self-destructiveness, against these proud and stupid ways of life, what counter-force can be set in motion? Listen to the word of the dying Christ! Forgiveness, *forgiveness.* Perhaps we should hasten to find another word, for I fear we have drained that one until it has become purely passive. For us to forgive is to look the other way, to pretend we did not feel it, to dismiss it as not having been very important anyway. For us, forgiveness has come so close to meaning accepting another man's apology that we cannot take it very seriously.

How can we recover our lost sense of the dynamic quality of forgiveness? Did you ever stop to think that in the Apostles' Creed, only one word is spoken about the whole of Christian existence, only one word used to describe the actual out-working of the Christian ethic? I believe in the forgiveness of sins. This is the motivating force that makes a Christian style of life possible. This is the drive that makes us move out into a disordered world with confidence and assurance. This is the power, we are convinced— and convinced because we have felt its power—the power that can change and transform any situation. The only power that Jesus Christ knew that was capable of redeeming those who in their blind folly were destroying themselves as they thought to destroy him. *Father, forgive them, for they know not what they do.*

We had a little illustration of it, just a beginning, in our city after Dr. King's assassination. I refer not only to the calm in which we were able to live while other cities all around us were exploding. I refer to that mass of people black and white together, who walked through the slums of Newark on Palm Sunday. Many of these people not so very long ago were frightened to death of each other, were spreading all kinds of rumors about each other, were sworn to see that one or the other had to go. And the plain truth is that they didn't know what they were doing. In their panic to protect themselves and their positions, they were perilously close to destroying an entire community.

I know how scared some people were to go on that walk that Palm Sunday. But I also know how powerful the force of forgiveness was once it began to make itself felt in that crowd of people. I am not so naïve as to claim that that's the solution to the whole problem. But I am claiming that we have been pointed in a new direction, given a new motivation, enriched with new strength and new power.

Yes, and I am claiming that the new direction, the new motivation, the new strength and power all come finally from this cross. All that Jesus had said about the power of forgiveness is here gathered up and hurled as one last defiant challenge at a world which can accept nothing but destruction. Do not think of this word as the passive acceptance of a situation for which there was no alternative. Think of it rather as the banner under which our Christ invades the heart of the hurt of the world—and summons us to follow. *Father, forgive them, for they know not what they do.*

12

The Second Word-1968

And he said unto Jesus, Lord, remember me when thou comest into thy kingdom. And Jesus said unto him, Verily, I say unto thee, Today thou shalt be with me in paradise.
Luke 23:43

I cannot get it out of my head that the last request of this dying man to the dying Jesus was, "Remember me." Religious tradition presents him to us as the "penitent thief," but I am not at all sure how accurate a description of him that is. He was hanging there on the cross because he was a militant, a revolutionary, one of the thousands of zealots in the Israel of that day who had vowed to bring down the rule of Rome at any price. He may have looted and he may have burned, but his motivation for these acts had been his dedication to his people's freedom. That was why he was hanging there as our Lord's companion in death. For Rome dealt with such people severely whenever it could lay hands upon them.

Yes, and though it may seem shocking, I should like to question his penitence. To be sure, Luke records a certain admission on his part that, given the rules of the game, he belonged where he was, as opposed to Jesus whom they had hung there without reason. But that is hardly penitence. Nor is his cry to Jesus a cry of penitence either. "Forgive me, I am deeply sorry"—this was not the kind of word that came from his lips. No, I seem to hear a certain pride in his plea. "Sir, remember me; remember me."

The more you stop to think about it, the more you begin to realize that all of humanity's woe echoes in that cry, "Remember me." For what this man was asking at the very least (I agree there is more) was to be met and noticed and remembered as a human person. All his life long he had been struggling against a system that had been organized to degrade him, to drain him of his humanity, to rob him of his dignity. His burning and his looting were not only protests against that system, they were desperate attempts to win the kind of recognition and attention that he felt he had been denied. All his life long he had been in active revolt against a system that had treated him and his family like slaves, denying him the basic decencies of humanity. And now even in death he was being denied them. There was to be no dignity in his dying, but he was to be nailed up on display like a bat on a barn door.

What was it do you suppose that made him realize in those last few painful hours of life that the man dying next to him was different from the system? It is, of course, impossible to say whether he had ever heard of Jesus before death brought them together. From the placard hanging over the head of the man on the central cross, as well as from all the hooting and jeering below, he realized that here too was some kind of revolutionary. "The King of the Jews," it said. Had he also heard the word of forgiveness spoken earlier? Had he had time to become aware of the calm dignity of this man who was dying like a king, with no word of rebellion or frustration on his lips?

As to the cause we can only speculate. As to the result we can be certain. This was a man who even in death would recognize him as a brother, a man who would understand and accept his humanity, mistaken and broken as it might have been. This was a man with whom one could walk into that long dark tunnel with no light at the end and feel confidence in his understanding and acceptance. The other revolutionary on the other cross had cursed him, challenged him, and he had taken the cursing and accepted the challenge in a wonderfully understanding silence. This was then the man who could give him, even at this final moment, the thing for which he had been searching his whole life and never really found—the sense that he was accepted as a human being. "Sir, remember me."

I must pause here long enough to point out to what an extent in our society it is still the same. Whether the person be locked in one of our great corporations and feels like nothing more than an IBM card or whether the person be locked in one of our ghettos feeling nameless, the desire to be recognized, met, and known as a human being is still a strong one. I should not hesitate to say that the inhumanity of many of the situations in urban areas, the brutality, the violence, are only the outward signs of a people who feel that they no longer have any humanity but are case loads, card files, pieces to be shoved around on the chess board of power struggles. *Remember me, remember me* is the bitter cry of the lost who are lost because they are no longer really sure that they are human.

And how does Jesus reply to us? By the simple assurance that we are remembered and that we will be remembered, that we are accepted and that we will be accepted. *Today thou shalt be with me in paradise.* In that place of beauty and peace where we wait for God to complete the revolution, for God to establish the kingdom, we shall be together. For now we are brothers and sisters, children of that Father whose heart is so great that not one can go beyond its love, a love which is so vast that no one ever goes unnoticed or is forgotten. And although the record does not state it, I am convinced that that man died with a dignity which he had never been able to find in life.

It was, of course, the wonder of our Lord's earthly life and ministry that he was always able to do this. He made them believe that they were somebody. Whether it was the woman taken in adultery, the widow dropping her pennies in the collection box, or the blind beggar by the side of the road to Jericho, they were always persons. We should not be surprised to discover, therefore, that even in the agony of dying, Jesus' way was still the same. Other men looking at that cross where this man hung said, "Brigand, thief, subversive." Jesus said, "Brother, let us walk together into whatever awaits us."

And I make bold to point out that he did so here, as he always did in life, without any long questionnaire as to previous activities, without any determination as to the worthiness of the case, without any demand or pre-condition (tell me you are sorry and we will see what we can do). All of the fussy moralisms and religious niceties which we so often try to wind around the heart of God meant nothing to Jesus. They never had; they did not now. *Remember me.* I tell you we shall be together in God's beauty, God's goodness, God's love.

No, it is not surprising that this was Jesus on his cross when it had been Jesus all his life long. But what is surprising and saddening is the community of his disciples. I am speaking now to myself and to you. Have you ever said, speaking about certain groups of people in our society, "Well, they must first prove themselves and then we'll see what can be done." "But I think they ought to earn some things before they have things given to them." Have you ever spoken like that, thought like that? Can you really stand at the foot of the cross at this moment and still speak like that, still think like that?

For what is the task of the Christian community in our community if it is not to infiltrate an inhuman and dehumanizing world as the people who are willing to accept a person as a person and treat that person as a human being? What has happened to us that that community which our Lord called into being as the community of acceptance has become the community of rejection and of judgment? Some little time ago I was speaking with a young lady from my city who had been a drug addict and had spent some time in the County Jail because of her habit. I asked her what had persuaded her to give it up. Was it psychiatry or social rehabilitation or one of our numerous agencies. She looked at me as though she thought I was stupid. "I just met somebody up there in the jail," she replied, "who cared about me."

About *me*. Not about my habit, about my addiction, about my criminal record, but just about me, about me as a person. *Remember me*. It was the cry of the dying revolutionary; it is the cry of the wasted young person in the ghetto, the ADC mother in a housing project, the old man living by himself in a furnished room, the rising young executive in a downtown office—*remember me*. And we live in a society which isn't built to remember, doesn't know how to remember, doesn't want to remember.

But Jesus did. And he expects us to be able to do the same—or to give up using his name in vain. Do you remember that wonderful line in Samuel Beckett's novella, *Dante and the Lobster*, when the despondent young man cries out, "My God, why can't people have less piety and more pity?" Why can't we stop talking about paradise and start bringing significance to the insignificant, humanity to the dehumanized, concern to the forgotten? Or what's Good Friday all about anyway? *Sir, remember me. Today thou shalt be with me in paradise.*

13

The Third Word-1968

*When Jesus therefore saw his mother and the disciple
standing by whom he loved, he saith unto his mother,
Woman, behold thy son! Then saith he to the disciple,
behold thy mother! And from that hour, that disciple
took her unto his own home.*
John 19:26-27

Now what was Jesus doing at this point? At first sight it does seem like rather a strange business! He was obviously arranging a home for his mother, making sure that she was provided for by entrusting her welfare to the responsibility of his close friend, John. But Mary already had a home. There were other brothers and sisters in the family and, if the facts be known, the main burden of Mary's support had fallen on them for some little time now. After all, his public career had taken Jesus away from home for months if not for years. And while I cannot believe that he had not made some contribution to her welfare during that time, still it cannot be denied that her home had been with the rest of the family. What then is the reason for this sudden new arrangement made in the very last hours of his life?

I have no desire to sit in judgment upon the other members of Jesus' family. But I have to be honest and tell you that the record states that they had not been a sympathetic lot. Once they had tried to persuade him to come home. Of course, they tried to put the best possible face on it and say that he was tired, over-worked, and that sort of thing. But reading between the lines, it is easy to see that the real reason for their sudden show of apparent concern was the simple fact that he was embarrassing them by his speech and by his actions. Frankly, they were ashamed to admit that he belonged to them. But since they could hardly deny it, the best thing was to get him home and keep him locked up in the living room or at least some place where they could keep a watchful eye on his activities.

Of course, their attempt failed. But it is indication enough that while Mary had a home she did not have a home. Bread and soup and salt might be on the table, a roof over her head, a pillow on which to rest her head at night. But love and sympathy and understanding were not among the comforts provided by that home in Nazareth. I wonder. Do you suppose that Jesus visualized her having to go back there after this awful day was over to sit listening to their spiteful, "We told you so." "If only he had listened to us when we tried to persuade him."? It isn't an easy thing, you know, to have had a brother who was crucified. It makes it pretty hard to hold up your head when you walk down the street. It is difficult not to hate him for the shame he has brought to you. No, back to that she could not go. *"Woman, behold! Thy son. Behold thy mother." And from that hour that disciple took her unto his own home.*

Again it is nothing new. He had said it many times during his life. But I think we need to think for a few moments about the high value which Jesus Christ placed on significant human relationships, the way in which he realized the need that people have for other people, not merely in casual acquaintance but in deep levels of meaning. For one reason or another we have tended to assume that the family relationship takes care of all this kind of thing. And, to be sure, it often does. But as in our Lord's own case, there are also times when it doesn't. In our society, we should be distressingly familiar with these.

It is a cliché to point to the deterioration of family life as one of the contributing causes of our sickness. Detailed studies have been carried on to prove it, as you doubtless know. For my part, I regret that these studies were limited to a particular kind of family situation in the urban ghetto, for I suspect that a similar study of family life in the good middle-class suburb would not have revealed a picture that was much more encouraging.

The result has been that in our day there are great efforts to restore and rebuild the efficacy of the family as a significant unit in human relations. I'm all for them. Who could be against them? But I find myself wondering whether that's where we have to stop, we Christians. I find myself wondering whether in this day of broken homes, shattered relationships, and fragmented persons, our responsibilities do not run much deeper than sending a contribution to the local Family Service Agency and wishing it well in its Christmas appeal.

I have always been somewhat puzzled by that popular song from the movie, *Funny Girl*: "People who need people are the luckiest people in the world." In my experience people who need people are often the unluckiest people in the world because they can't find people, because their need for significant and meaningful relationships is a great aching hunger that it is impossible for them to satisfy. People who will sell them things, people who will collect bills from them, people who will ask them to join their organization, people who will hand them a check, people who will make sure that the rent is paid or send them a food order—these they have in great abundance. But they want something more and that they do not know where to find.

I think this is what lay behind our Lord's rearrangement of his mother's domestic situation. He knew who would see that she didn't starve to death or walk around the streets in rags. But he also knew that the human spirit needs something more than that, needs love, understanding, sympathy, an ear to listen and a shoulder to cry on. And that, briefly stated, was why he took her out of Nazareth and sent her to live with John. She needed more than board and room—she needed people.

Now it should be obvious to us that this is what a congregation is for, that this new grouping of brothers and sisters in Christ has no greater task than to provide that kind of supportiveness, that kind of meaningful friendship for each other. In the life of the congregation we should be beholding new sons and new mothers all the time. Certainly it cannot be denied that this was the appeal of the Christian congregation once it got loose in the world. In a world which, like ours, had no time for anybody, here was a group of people who were serious about their responsibilities to each other, whose sorrows and joys, whose problems and pains were things that they all held in common.

I should like to think that that were still the case, but I have to say that I know better. It is amazing to me how little people know what is happening to their brothers and sisters in Christ. It is sad to think, even when they do know, how little they care. I have been told that there is more genuine friendliness in the corner tavern than there is in the typical Protestant congregation. I confess to no firsthand experience, but I think it may be possible.

And I think that this lies at the root of our Christian ineffectiveness in the world. We are forever being urged from the pulpit to get out there in the world and show that we care. But the plain truth is that we don't know how to do it because we don't know how to do it in the Church where it is supposed to be happening. If I understand the New Testament correctly, any congregation is supposed to be a sample, a display to the world of what the world could be like if it accepted Jesus Christ as Lord. Well, honestly now, do you really wonder why the world shows little interest in what we have to offer?

Yet how can we deny that what Jesus Christ wants to do with us is to place us in new positions of responsibility and concern, to integrate our brokenness into new patterns of meaning? Many of you who are reading this page are probably members of a Christian congregation in which you have all kinds of brothers and sisters, even though you may be the last of your family. These possibilities for meaningful and exciting community have been given to us in this theatre of new and creative relationships which we call the Church. In that older woman who lives by herself we are asked to see our mother. In that young man who is all mixed up and doesn't know quite where he is going, we are shown our son.

And if I hear what our Lord is saying to us from his cross, he is asking us to go out and find them, to translate into reality the new relationships which he has made possible. For we must never forget that the key to the relationship is our relationship with him. Jesus is, so to speak, the head of the family and it is only because we are all related to him that we are related to each other.

The family of God—here at the foot of the cross is its beginning as Mary goes home with John. And here it is in its fullness as people of all kinds gather together on Good Friday to celebrate his cross and passion. We are not so many individuals but kinfolk, a family. But how can we ever hope to persuade the world to join the family until we have found each other in honesty, seriousness, and love? *Woman, behold thy son! Behold thy mother!*

14

The Fourth Word-1968

My God, my God,
Why hast thou forsaken me?
  Matthew 27:46, Mark 15:34

If I am at all accurate as an observer of the theological scene, we seem to be emerging today from that rather brief year in which so many people were fascinated by the lapidary announcement: God is dead. I have seen no national news magazine running the divine obituary on its cover page as *Time* did some while back. I see fewer and fewer sermon titles that make use of the phrase. Indeed I suspect that the sale of the three or four books which discussed this proposition has fallen off markedly in the past few months. Part of this, of course, is due to the fact that once you have said that God is dead, there isn't much to say except that God is deader. And that doesn't make a great deal of sense. But more importantly, I think, is the fact that we have begun to re-examine the validity of the proposition itself, begun to ask whether what seemed to us as God being dead may not have been one of the striking signs of the mysterious ways in which God is alive.

All that certainly is relevant when we consider this fourth word from the cross. If in this moment of exquisite torment Jesus Christ

had cried, "God is Dead," who really could have blamed him? Was
there really any evidence at that point for God's being alive, or if
alive, for being at all concerned or involved with the world God had
claimed to create? The dream of a lifetime had been shattered; the
mission and the calling seemed to have been frustrated and defeated.
All there was to show for it was a couple of emotional women. The
pain was unbearable, but more unbearable still was the howling of
the mob, the taunts and jeers of the establishment pounding Jesus
with the stabbing reminders of his failure, his defeat, his disgrace.
If at that moment he had summoned up his little remaining strength
and said, "I was cheated and defrauded. The God in whose name
I preached obviously does not exist. The God in whose name I
labored is dead." If that had been his final word, who could have
blamed him?

There are those who believe that this is essentially what Jesus was
saying at this point, and I hope I am not employing subtle
distinctions when I tell them that they are wrong. It is one thing to
say, "God is dead," but it is quite another to say, "My God, why hast
thou forsaken me." You see the difference, I am sure. When Jesus
said, "My God," he was addressing a living person. And when he
asked the reason for the abandonment, he was accusing his God of
a definite action. His question was why, at that particular moment,
God had hidden himself from him.

I want to make that as clear as I can because I think it is so terribly
important in our time of apparent hopelessness and despair. Jesus
Christ never for one moment doubted that somewhere in the
hopelessness and despair, his God was at work. It was like calling
to someone in a pitch black cave. He knew God was there and was
doing something. Why couldn't God give him a little measure of
comfort and assurance? Why did God suddenly have to go incognito,
so to speak, and carry on without a sound, without a whisper, with
nothing to indicate his presence. *My God, my God, why hast thou
forsaken me?*

I hasten to add that there is no answer to such a question. Reverently I say that not even the blessed Savior himself received an answer. I do not know why it is that some times God chooses to work in the dark. But I want to hold up as clearly as I can before you the Good Friday faith of Jesus Christ, that even in the darkest darkness, God does work. The darkness in which there is no sound is not a sign that God is dead but mysteriously alive. Us, God may leave comfortless and alone. God's work and purposes are never forsaken. The agony in him could force Jesus to ask why God had forsaken him. But no agony could force Jesus to ask why God had forsaken his purpose for his world.

I think I know perhaps as well as anyone the bitter frustrations, the agonizing disappointments of trying to live and work in the midst of a city. I don't know which is more bitter or frustrating, the indifference of the people who ought to care or the violence of the people who do care. There are so many of our social problems, so many of our community woes on which God simply seems to have walked out and left nobody in charge. Have you never wanted to say, "It just doesn't make any difference; no matter what I do or how I act or what position I take. It just doesn't make any difference. The thing always seems to turn out wrong. What's the good of it anyway? Preacher, you always tell us about goodness and mercy, about love and kindness. But does God know about these things? Is God as concerned about them as you are or as you want to be? Maybe you should tell God about them because he certainly has a way of fading whenever they are in question."

I'll agree that God has a way of leaving us wondering, for I have been left wondering more times than one. God left Jesus wondering. But never once did Jesus, even while he wondered, doubt the integrity of the Father's purpose, the goodness of his will. And that's what mattered. That's what brought Jesus through. That's what made his last word a word of confidence and not a word of doubt.

I know that I am not asking an easy thing when I ask you in days such as these to stay resolutely with what you believe when there seems to be absolutely nothing in it for you. I know I am not asking an easy thing when I ask that in the midst of our disorder and upheaval you continue to put it on the line, even when the price is high and the threat of danger is real. But I am asking a deeply Christian thing. I am asking the thing that Jesus Christ did on his cross in his time of abandonment. All his life he had been speaking out plainly. Even while he spoke out plainly, he realized that some day he might be called upon to pay up personally. Now that day had come and the price was high. But he paid it, even when he felt all alone, he paid it because he believed in what he had said.

Let me point out one thing to you which must be said because we can never separate Good Friday from Easter. There on the cross in Jesus' aloneness he refused to allow his aloneness to destroy his faith that his Father was at work in the dark. And that faith was justified. Easter was not a happy ending in which Prince Charming was rescued. There could have been no Easter without the cross. But how could anyone have known that these three hours of torment and pain were necessary if darkness was to turn to light and death to life, anyone except God in the secret and mysterious working of his being?

My God, why hast thou forsaken me? So it may seem; so it may seem. But you and I and the world in which we live are all part of God's great intention for reconciliation and righteousness. He has not forsaken these, no, not even when we try to drive God out and let our way take over. I hesitate to say that the violence and the upheavals of this day are signs that God has not forsaken his purpose and intention. But you know, they may be. Perhaps there is just no other way left by which a world that has become smug and complacent in its comfort and its affluence can be jolted into the recognition of reality. Perhaps there is no other way in which a sick society can be restored to health except by drastic surgery. It may be hard for us to realize that in so many of the frightening noises of our day God's truth is marching on. But it could be.

You know, I am sure, that this word of abandonment is a quotation from the Twenty-second Psalm, its opening line in fact. Jesus knew the Psalms, knew every word of every one of them. Do you suppose that having identified himself with the psalmist in his cry of lostness, "My God, my God, why hast thou forsaken me?" he went on identifying himself with the rest of the psalm? "All the ends of the world shall remember and turn unto the Lord; all the kindreds of the nations shall worship before thee. For the kingdom is the Lord's and he is the governor among the nations." I think so. And I think it was because even in Jesus' agony that psalm helped him see the glory of that kingdom which is the Lord's and the vision of its final triumph. And I think when he died, the loneliness was gone and the victory was there. God had not forgotten him but was using him, using even the dark mystery of his pain and suffering for the victory of his kingdom.

My God, my God, why hast thou forsaken me? But the kingdom is the Lord's, and mine eyes have seen its glory.

15

The Fifth Word-1968

I thirst.
　　John 19:28

How strangely these words from the cross follow each other! A few moments ago we were thinking about a word which really took us deep into the heart of God. And now comes one which is simple and almost pathetic in its physical need. "I thirst." It is almost as though having struggled to satisfy the deep needs of his spirit Jesus now became aware of the needs of his body. In fact, it is interesting to note in passing how little is said in the gospel stories about the needs of his body. This is the only reference, "I thirst."

Well, you may well ask, "How do you preach a sermon on a thing like that?" The dying Christ was thirsty. Somebody from the crowd stepped up and moistened those parched lips. And then the curtain falls and the little episode is ended. What can we say? It is, of course, a poignant reminder that the Christ whom we worship was a real human being and not the bloodless theological figure that we so often make him, a poignant reminder that he shared human existence out to the full, exempt from none of its needs. And surely the recognition of that fact is an important one for the humanity of

Jesus which is something that so many of us find so difficult really to accept.

But that humanity of Jesus, especially as glimpsed here in this little episode, has so much wider and deeper dimensions than we commonly realize. We all recall the word he said on another occasion. "Come, ye blessed of my Father, for I was thirsty and ye gave me to drink." And when the startled hearers replied, "Lord, when did we see thee thirsty and gave thee to drink?" he said, "Inasmuch as ye did it unto one of the least of these my brethren, ye did it unto me." We all recall it, I say. But do we really think it through? Let's try for these few moments.

I should like to begin by asking a question which may at first strike you as having little to do with the case. What is the motivation for our service in the places of need in our community? Why should we be out there anyway doing things? I suspect that had we the time to garner some answers to that question on Good Friday, honest answers, not conventionally pious ones, we should find a startling variety. Some might reply that in service of this kind we discover new significance and meaning in life for ourselves. Some might even admit that their reason for being there and doing things is simply that if somebody doesn't do them, there is likely to be trouble which will prove more costly and more bothersome in the end.

But I suspect there would be few, if any, who would say, "I must go to these places and to these people because that is where Jesus Christ is." I have mentioned before the dehumanizing of people in our culture. Now will you think for a moment about the dehumanizing of Jesus Christ in our religion? Instinctively we feel that to go where Jesus Christ is means going to church, to some religiously suggestive place where the world is closed out and our hearts can be tuned in on other things.

But that is not how the gospel reads. "I was thirsty and you gave me a drink." They did not meet him, these blessed of the Father, in the pomp and circumstance of a liturgical ceremony, but in the basic

physical need of someone else. In a real sense, his humanity still
continues. He who cried from the cross, "I thirst," is still crying with
a thousand voices for the same simple ministry of that unnamed
man who stepped from the crowd and moistened his lips.

Hunger, thirst, nakedness—the most elemental demands of
simple human existence—do you wonder that Archbishop Temple
once described Christianity as the most materialistic of all the
world's great religions? This is where the concern of Christian
people begins and must begin. And don't be put off by the silly
assertion that we need not worry any longer because the government
is taking care of such things. I can assure you quite differently. I
know that there are all kinds of other good things which we can and
we must bring to people. We are something more than an
ecclesiastical welfare agency. That is perfectly true. But we are a
failure as a church when we are something less, when we kid
ourselves into thinking that ours is the fairly painless responsibility
of looking after souls while somebody can have the dirty job of
looking after their bodies.

And let me say right here that when we talk about thirst and
hunger and nakedness in the gospel terms, we are talking about
many things beside. We are talking about bad housing and bad
plumbing. We are talking about dirty streets and filthy alleys. We are
talking about poor medical facilities and sparse opportunities for
dental care. We are talking about unsafe places to play or no places
to play at all. I know we don't enjoy talking about these things. I
know some of us don't think that they are very religious and that
preachers ought to talk about nicer things.

But you see, such subjects are deeply religious. They lie as close
to the heart of the gospel as anything I could think of. But let's put
them in their right context. Jesus Christ is living in those slums,
playing in those dirty alleys, waiting for someone to check up on his
health. And all of the business we do with him here in the church,
though I grant you it is not without its importance, is hollow and
empty unless it motivates us to do business with him there. For the

final judgment will not be based on the regularity of our church attendance or the size of our contribution. The final judgment will be based on the seriousness with which we answered the cries of the needy, the hungry, the thirsty. For these are really the cries of Christ. *I thirst.*

And I have to say to you in all candor that I am depressed by the relatively few members of the church who get themselves involved in this kind of thing. So often the person who is there in response to the need is the secular person. I don't honestly suppose it was a priest or a scribe who stepped out of the crowd that day to give the dying Christ something with which to moisten his lips. It was just a person. And maybe one of the reasons why God's beloved community seems to be failing in the world is just here, that we have not really seen where our Lord is and what it is that he is asking us to do.

Perhaps something else is true here also. I have the suspicion, at least, that for many of us it is difficult to know Jesus as a living reality. The figure from ancient history or the wise teacher whose voice still echoes strongly from the past, these figures we understand. But we are mystified when we hear about the living presence and often try to excuse our failure by saying that we are not mystics. But where is this living presence to be found? Not, I am sure, in mystical visions, though they come to some, but in the place where he promised his presence—in the activity of serving the least and the last and the lost, in answering the cry of the thirsty with the cup of cold water given in his name—there we find him.

I can think of no more powerful good a vigil by the cross on Good Friday can do for us than to enlarge our ideas of spirituality and make us aware of our real calling to serve the Christ who lives incognito. Even as we are reading these words, Jesus is still thirsting. Should we remain unaware of that or unconcerned about it, we shall really have missed the whole point of the story. But if this cry from the cross stabs us into the realization of who he really is and who they are that need us, then the power of his cross will still be strong to save.

It was a simple act when someone stepped from the crowd to do what could be done to answer a cry of need. But do you remember that wonderful story about Phillips Brooks and the fashionable lady who asked him to suggest to her an appropriate lenten devotion? His suggestion was that she come to a home in a South Boston slum and help with the washing and cleaning. For a while she resisted the suggestion, but one day she ordered her carriage and reluctantly went. Nervously climbing the tenement stairs, she feebly tapped at the door, only to hear the booming voice of her rector inside, "Come on in, sister, I've been expecting you." When finally we take the step and do that simple act, we shall hear the voice of the Lord Christ himself, whom we have sought perhaps and never really found saying, "Come on in, my brother, my sister, I've been expecting you." *I thirst.*

16

The Sixth Word-1968

It is finished!
  John 19:30

And please do not think that this dying cry from the lips of Jesus Christ was the final gasp of a worn out and defeated man who was creeping off the stage of life, broken and defeated. The evangelists make it perfectly clear that it was the great shout of achievement from one who knows that he has done it, the full-throated cry of the conqueror. The enemy has been driven back and is now in full retreat. The invader has sent wave after wave against him but could not capture the fortress of his spirit. Not even the doubt which for a moment seemed to have taken possession could permanently hold what it had gained. Jesus had been entrusted with the command to obey and to continue to obey even to the end of the end and he had done it. *It is finished.*

I pause here long enough to ask that if you have never thought of the cross in this way you reconsider your opinion for a moment. Too many of us, I fear, have been accustomed to thinking of the cross in passive terms. There hangs the helpless martyr who commands our sorrow and our sympathy. Jesus Christ never asked for sorrow or sympathy. If there is any weeping to be done, he said to the women following him as he walked up Calvary's hill, please don't weep for me. Weep for yourselves and for your children! Look again and keep on looking until you see that this man is not the helpless martyr but the glorious victor who has won his right to rule human life by refusing to be victimized by all of the bitter and shameful and harsh things that despoil it. They tried and they failed and now it is finished. "O Sacred Head Now Wounded" has become "Glory, Glory, Hallelujah!"

I think that this is important because I believe that we all are under the same commitment to obey and to keep on obeying until the end of the end, that we all are under the obligation so to live out our days, so to act out our faith that when our call comes we too can say, "It is finished," and say it not in the sense of "I've had it" but in the sense of Paul: "I have fought the good fight; I have finished the course." You see the similarity between Paul and his Master. But we should see the same similarity between us and our Master as well.

Not that I am suggesting that there will not be failures and defeats in our record even as Paul would have been the first to admit that there were in his. But the power to pick ourselves up from the defeat and start moving once again in the same direction, the grace to acknowledge the failure and in the assurance of forgiveness to move on once more toward the achievement of the purpose—this is the strange wonder of the Christian gospel, this is the power of the cross. Just when we are scared away and say, "No, it is impossible; we cannot stay here any longer," we are overshadowed by the presence of him who said, "It is finished." Or to use those wonderful words of Dr. Tyrell's, "What a relief if one could conscientiously wash one's hands of the whole concern. But then there is that Strange Man upon His Cross who drives one back again and again."

But there is much more involved here even than that. Since we have been meditating on the cross under the oppressive shadow of what has been called "the urban crisis," let's think about it for a moment. In most of our congregations there are probably all kinds of opinions about it. But varied as these opinions might be, in one thing I am certain we should all agree. It is a mess; it is a first class mess. Where do you begin to tackle it? Which end should you try to pick up first? What will make the slightest dent in it? And if you have tried to do even the littlest thing about it, you will know how quickly you can get shot down, how easily you can be told that you are doing the wrong thing, how angry the reprisals can be.

I am sure that in this crisis the Christian forces are as badly paralyzed as they are partly because a lot of us need to have our ideas lifted until we see what is really going on, because a lot of us are trying to live in a past which is irrevocably gone. But I am sure that another great reason for our paralysis is the simple fact that we are afraid to move in any direction because we are not sure what the consequences may be, not sure whether our moves will get anywhere if we make them. And so we stand on the sidelines wringing our hands and saying, "Isn't it terrible?" But nothing happens because we don't know how to make it happen.

Well, if I have caught the mood of some of us at least, let me speak to it in this way. The only solution to the urban crisis is the kingdom of God and you know what that means as well as I do. All we have to do is to find the particular point at which it is our task to translate that kingdom into some form of specific action. It will be costly. It may involve rejection; it may involve defeat. You may come home more than once and say, "What's the use? I'm not getting anywhere. I make more enemies than friends by taking the stand that I do. I'm getting knocked on the head and slapped in the face for positions that I believe are right. Why should I be bothered any longer?"

Right there, friend, stop and remember, *it is finished.* Because of this tremendous victory on the cross which you and I celebrate on Good Friday, the question no longer is whether or not the kingdom of God will come. That question has been settled and it will never be re-opened. *It is finished.* All power is now in those nail-pierced hands. The only question remaining to be answered is where you are and where I am. Are we in or out? Are we standing with the kingdom or against it? Are we serving it or are we serving something else? And let me point out with all the force at my command that sitting on our hands while mouthing pretty pious phrases is serving something else; saying "Lord, Lord" out of one corner of the mouth while saying "these people" out of the other is serving the kingdom of hell. Don't fool yourself.

But realists that we all like to be, we want to say, "Come now, where is that kingdom or even a sign of that kingdom in the urban crisis? We can easily see the signs of all kinds of power plays and evil designs. We can readily detect the evidence that all kinds of wicked men are using this dreadful situation for their own selfish purposes. But where is the sign of the kingdom? Are we not being asked to serve something that doesn't exist?"

So back we go to the cross and to this wonderful word, *it is finished.* What else can you make out of it but this? We are summoned and sent to serve that which has already happened. Our task is to make people know that it has happened. Not for one moment can we doubt that when the last chapter has been written the kingdom of God will be there in all its glory in Newark, Detroit, Chicago, or Washington. Why else do we pray, "Thy kingdom come, thy will be done on earth as it is in heaven"? We can labor and know that we are not laboring in vain. We can be steadfast and know that our stance is not a foolish one. We can be immovable and know that not even the tides of hatred and prejudice can move us because we are servants of that which is already here, against which the very things that were powerless to defeat him must also be powerless to defeat us also. *It is finished.*

To give St. Augustine's remark a modern translation, "Even when everything else falls apart, the cross stands fixed and firm." In this turbulent and chaotic world, there is our fixed point of reference. Because it could not happen there, it cannot finally happen anywhere. There will be crosses again and again. Truth may be standing on the scaffold for what may seem to be most of history.

But do not be deceived by the appearances. Above all, do not let them lead your life into the distortions of compromise. Because of this cross, these crosses, our crosses, will finally be validated. Because of this cross, that scaffold holds the future. All we can go out into the world of the urban crisis, go out into any world, and take it because now we know it like it really is. The battle has been won. All that has been left to us are the mopping up operations. *It is finished.*

And now a little postscript. I am sure that when our history has been written, the murder of Martin Luther King will prove to be one of the turning points. I don't know of any man who believed as implicitly what I have tried to say. This is what he meant, I am sure, when he said the night before he died that he had been on the mountaintop and seen the promised land. O, my brothers and sisters, we could all be there and we could all have the same vision because the promised land has already been won for us. Just have the courage to stand up and look forward. *It is finished.*

17

The Seventh Word-1968

Father, into thy hands I commend my spirit.
Luke 23:46

...and so he bowed his head and died. But that's not what I want us to think about as we prepare to leave the foot of his cross. Of course, it was a magnificent way to die, so wonderful that, as you probably know, the phrase has passed over into any number of Christian liturgies and been used times without end by the followers of Jesus Christ as they prepared to leave this world. There is a Christian art of dying and it all began here at the cross as the Savior of mankind himself prepared to leave this world. "Father, into thy hands I commend my spirit."

But the important thing for us to notice about this farewell word of Jesus is the fact that it is the perfect summary of the way he had lived. In fact it would be difficult to think of words which more completely and more perfectly described his outlook on the meaning of life than these. *Father, into thy hands I commend my spirit.* Basically a quotation from one of the psalms, in common use as part of the evening prayer of all devout Jewish families, to say nothing of the service of evening prayer in the Temple itself, these are words that

Jesus Christ had sought to act out at least from the time that he was a boy of twelve. That his life, his experience, his activity, his dying all were in the hands of his Father, that was his central conviction, a conviction which not even the ravages of three hours upon the cross had been able in any way to alter. "Do you not know that I must be about my Father's business?" That was where he began. "Father, into thy hands I commend my spirit." That was where he ended. The opening and closing statement of his understanding of the meaning of himself and of his life were the same—Father.

Face to face with the critical situation of our time, with a sickness of our society which could be a sickness unto death, have you ever asked yourself what is the final thing in which you believe, the one conviction, if there is one, that you would rather suffer for than surrender? I know it is difficult to answer a question like that when we have never really been put to any kind of a test about it. What we might answer in the calmness of abstract thought might prove to be something quite different from what we should answer when the decision was actually demanded of us. But whatever you think your answer might be, I want to put before you today the answer of our Lord Jesus Christ, an answer made in life and validated in death—Father.

Let me attempt to translate that answer into somewhat different terms. How easily and how often it can be and has been sentimentalized as it stands! What our Lord wants to say is that the ultimate reality of this world, beyond which, around which, it is just not possible to go, is concern, understanding, forgiveness, love. O, there are a whole cluster of words which could be used, but you see what I am trying to say. The power, the reality that are final are the power and the reality of God, made real and explicit in Jesus Christ.

And when our Lord invites us to commit our lives to this power, he is asking us to do something very specific. He is asking us to take these lives of ours, as he took that life of his, and lay them down squarely and unreservedly on this line, convinced that this is the only line that really and finally matters. *Father, into thy hands I commend my spirit* is not only an office for the dying, it is a committal service to be offered every day that we live as we must make decisions about fresh circumstances and new situations. Face to face with the challenges of whatever may be, he asks us to say, "Father, into thy hands I commend my spirit."

But please observe that we are not being asked to do this as the helpless victims of circumstance, as if to say, "I do not know what is ahead of me but for whatever it may be, I commend myself to the mercies of God." That, of course, is all very true, but not the very significant part of it. No, we are asked to do this in a way that is active and dynamic. Because I have been convinced by Jesus Christ, by his cross and resurrection, that this is the final reality, I commit myself to it wholeheartedly and unreservedly, in life and death, to be the active and obedient servant of that reality in all circumstances. Confronted by the temptation to be less than that, to do less than that, to find shortcuts or easy ways out, *Father, into thy hands I commend my spirit.* Shape it, renew it, strengthen it, keep it firm, resolute, and obedient until that day comes when I can surrender it totally in the life of the world to come.

Am I asked to join the easy affluent and the comfortable indifferent? *Father, into thy hands I commend my spirit.* Am I tempted to throw up the task and walk away from the problem? *Father, into thy hands I commend my spirit.* Am I inclined to say, "The hell with it all" because hell is all any of it deserves? *Father, into thy hands I commend my spirit.* Do I find myself thinking that it is not really my problem and that therefore there is no reason why I should get myself involved? *Father, into thy hands I commend my spirit.* Am I considering the strong possibility that the world may be right after all and this Christian thing so much starry-eyed dreaming? *Father, into thy hands I commend my spirit.* Have I caught the vision of the cross which they have prepared for me and started to move in the other direction as fast as I can decently go? *Father, into thy hands I commend my spirit.* Where is the ultimate commitment of your life, and if it is not here, then who are you anyway?

But these hands of God into which we commend our spirits are not just great big empty things waiting to catch us as one by one we drop off the map of the universe. The hands of God from the beginning have been and continue to be creative hands, hands which can never stay idle but must always be making, remaking, changing, transforming. We cannot therefore commit ourselves into these hands and expect to be the same again. For the moment we fall into their control, we begin to experience their strength to change. Old people are made new; cynical and despairing people are transformed into prisoners of hope; the hate is worked out of us, the bitterness seared away, replaced by love and kindness. Our committal to these hands not only gives us our task but makes us more able for our task as the hands of God reshape us into what we were meant to be. *Father, into thy hands* is not only commitment, it is new creation.

But, of course, it is something more. It is confidence and courage. For he's got the whole world in his hands. And because we have been cleansed by this cross, we can face even this world of urban crisis, confidently and courageously because we know that this is our Father's world. It is not the world of the white racist or the black militant, it is not the world of the slumlord or the price gouger, it is not the world of the police or the criminal,—he's got the whole world in his hands!

Because God has you and me in his hands also and only because of that, we can go into the world which frightens and terrifies and panics and work and labor and witness and stick it out. No, it's stronger than that. Because these are the hands into which we have placed ourselves, the recreative and redemptive hands of God, we must go into that world to be creative and redemptive in the name of Jesus Christ. Put on the helmet of salvation because you will have some rocks thrown at your head. Get out the sword of the Spirit because there are sharp battles to be fought. Gird yourself with truth because there are all kinds of lies waiting to trap you. But just remember in whose hands you are and already you will be able to hear the shout of victory.

And that shout is not really very far away. For if you have kept your Good Friday vigil, then you know that when you hear this last word of our Lord's, *Father, into thy hands I commend my spirit*, the first Easter Alleluia is already distantly sounding. O think of those mighty hands which are shaping the world into beauty, truth, and peace even now. Yes, think of those other hands which even now are engaging in destruction and conflict. But think also of those useless hands which sit calmly folded or lying limply at the side.

And then in this solemn moment ask yourself, really ask yourself this question, with whose hands are my hands joined?

Do you have the courage, the grace, the strength, the seriousness to say it now, and at last really mean it? *Father, into thy hands I commend my spirit.*

Part III

Christmas

18

Christmas I

Lord, now lettest thou thy servant depart in peace, according to thy word: for mine eyes have seen thy salvation.

Luke 2:29-30

Who said that and when did he say it? Why, it was said by an old priest named Simeon about whom we know almost nothing. He said it one day when a young Jewish peasant girl brought her first baby to him to be blessed. It was the Jewish custom when a baby boy was forty days old to take him to the temple in Jerusalem that both mother and son might be blessed. In bringing her son Jesus to Simeon on this occasion, Mary was simply fulfilling a more or less routine prescription of her religion. No doubt she expected it to be just that, a few words of blessing by the priest, the sacrifice of a pair of doves, and that was that. Hundreds of Jewish mothers had taken their sons to be blessed in this fashion. Perhaps on the very day on which Mary went, there was a long line of mothers waiting with their sons—mothers of all kinds, mothers of great wealth and influence, mothers in important families, mothers from town and country alike. In a crowd like that, no one would be very likely to notice a young girl from Galilee who had given birth to her baby in a stable!

Yet when Mary's turn came, something entirely unexpected happened. The old priest who was performing the service that day was weary with his duties. It had been a long day for a man over eighty. But as this young Jewish girl stepped before him, his heart leapt up within him, his eye brightened, and eagerly he stretched forth his arms to take her son and hold him fast in his embrace, while in a torrent of joy the words poured forth from his lips, "Lord, now lettest thou thy servant depart in peace, according to thy word; for mine eyes have seen thy salvation." Life for him had now reached its glorious climax and fulfillment. Now there is nothing more that he hopes, nothing more that he dreams, nothing more that he desires. For in his arms he holds the fulfillment of his hopes, the realization of his dreams, the answer to his desires. *Lord, now lettest thou thy servant depart in peace!*

Something else might have happened there that day, you know. Old Simeon, weary of life and its illusions, dulled by the mechanical routine of his existence, disappointed so many times, defeated so many times, might have taken that child in his arms and seen in him nothing more than one more Jewish baby brought to him to be blessed. He might have taken him, mumbling the prescribed words and offering the necessary sacrifice and just another job, going back home at the day's end with his hopes still not fulfilled, his dreams still not realized, his prayers still not answered. Certainly there was nothing in either the child or his mother to indicate that he was different in the slightest from any of the other children who had come there that day. He had no halo, no angel choirs heralding his approach, no pomp and circumstance surrounding him whatever. He was just a baby held in the arms of a young mother from the country! Who could have blamed Simeon if he had taken no notice of either mother or child that day?

Certainly not you and I. For somehow at Christmastime the thing that did happen to Simeon never does happen to us. At Christmas, we may not actually take the child in our arms, but we do just about everything else. We sing about him, we act out his story in plays and pageants, we send pictures of him to each other on cards, we hear sermons preached about him, we read and hear the story of his coming from the Bible. How many Christmases have you lived through? Ten, twenty, forty, sixty? And in every one of them everything has been done to bring the Christmas child close and near to you. Yet, not twenty-four hours after it is all over, we go back to pick up life just where we left it off, playing with the same old illusions, dreaming the same old dreams, hoping the same old hopes, living through the same old struggles, knowing the same old defeats. For each one of us next Tuesday, life will be going on as though nothing had happened, as though we had seen nothing, heard nothing, knew nothing.

But here in this story, something did happen. This old man did see something, did hear something, did know something which meant that from now on life could never be what it had been before. Whether he had ten days or ten years yet to live, from now on he could live in peace because he had seen. No longer the agony of unfulfilled hopes, no longer the struggle of unanswered desires, no longer the conflict of unrealized dreams. From all of that agony, from all of that struggle, from all of that conflict, he had been set free. What he had seen had ended the agony, terminated the struggle, finished the conflict. Now he could go in peace, walk in confidence, live in assurance. *Lord, now lettest thou thy servant depart in peace, according to thy word: for mine eyes have seen thy salvation.*

And that is the thing that has never happened to us. To be set free so that we may walk the rest of the way of our lives in peace—we do not know that experience. In a world like ours, we have no real tomorrow, only a number of coming days just like today, filled with the struggle for bread, the conflict for success, the striving for a little place in the sun. Time spins us around on its dreary cycle. We struggle to be born, we struggle to live, we struggle to keep from dying, and then we struggle to die. Is it any wonder that we are tired of life and that we cling to it as desperately as we do only because we are afraid to imagine what might come after it? How can you talk about going in peace, about living in peace when this very week every one of us must go back to the struggle, the conflict, the agony of keeping life going, the clash and the competition of holding a job and earning a living, the strain and the wear of keeping a home and meeting life's responsibilities?

That's why we need Christmas! Simeon saw it; why can't you and I? We come with the broken imperfection of our lives, showing the marks of strain and care, the signs of worry and struggle, and we say, "God, I cannot do it. I cannot live beyond the strife and the struggle. I cannot rest in confidence. I cannot find peace." And what is the reply? Does God say, "Well, I am sorry, but that is no concern of mine; you will simply have to do the best you can?" No. Does God say, "I will tell you the way you should live and then if you don't, I shall have to punish you?" No. At Christmas, this is what God says: "You can't? Well I can! Let me live life for you! Let me come where you are, go where you go, endure what you endure. Then, following me, you can go your way in peace." That's what Simeon saw; that's why he knew that the hopes and dreams of his life had been fulfilled. God has come to claim human life. In person God is here to lead us in the ways of peace and confidence.

> So the all-great were the all-loving too—
> So, through the thunder comes a human voice
> Saying, O heart I made, a heart beats here!
> Face my hands fashioned, see it in myself!

For what, after all, would it mean to be able to live out our lives in peace, deep inner assurance of spirit? What but this? I can live in peace, I can go my way down through the years unshaken and unafraid if I am sure of my goal, of my purpose, and sure that I have the power to get there. When those conditions are absent, then peace vanishes from life with them. For many of us, life has no goal, no purpose. We do not see its meaning. We do not know where we are going. It strikes us as the senseless succession of things that merely happen. Today, tomorrow, a year from now, a year ago—

it's all alike, driven cruelly by a blind fate. How can our pathways lie in peace when that is our outlook on life? What chance have we of overcoming life's struggle when each new day must drive us in one direction or another?

But there are others of us who have purposes and goals in life. Sometimes they are good, sometimes they are bad, sometimes they are low, sometimes they are high. They may be no more than winning a promotion in the office, but goals and purposes at least they are. But do we have the power to reach them? Aye, there's the rub! How often as we think they are within our grasp, they withdraw from us further and elude our reach. Then we get panicky and frightened. How can there be peace with that kind of a way of living? To go in peace through life we need goals and purposes and we need to know that we have the power to achieve them.

In the Christ who is born this day you find them both. Life now has a goal and it has a purpose. Christ is its goal and its purpose. To make your life like his, to be conformed after his pattern, molded into his mind, shaped after his spirit, formed into his likeness—that's what he came to do. That's your destiny in him—nothing short of that, nothing less than that. Not the destiny of the saints, the priests and the preachers, but your destiny. John Jones and Mary Brown, shake yourselves from the dust and dirt of life as you now are living it and come to the manger. In the cradle, on the cross, or in the Easter garden, so shall you be. That's why Jesus came—to put before you in terms which you can grasp and understand, in terms of a life like yours and mine the hope of our high calling. Only give up all of the lesser ambitions and trifling purposes that you have and start moving in his direction!

Well, you say, I simply can't live like that! What do you think I am anyway? I am not Jesus Christ. I'm just plain Jane or ordinary Bill. So you are, but if you think that is an excuse, then you don't know the full glory of Christmas. The goal, the dream, the hope, the purpose—yes, and the power to make them true. That's here also. The power not just to exist or get by, the power to become not merely a good person or a fine citizen, but the power to become a child of God. John Jones, child of God, that's God's Christmas gift to you. Christ is no will-o-the-wisp, haunting you on your way. His life has come among us to stay. You have only to link your life to his and that power will carry you along in perfect confidence to the goal, to the dream, to the victory. You can get up in the morning, facing the most trying circumstances, the most pressing needs. Yet you can say, "God in Christ has already lived this day for me and he will live it with me." You can say that and be sure of it because of what happened at Christmas. And with that kind of assurance, that kind of power, you can go and face that day and every day in peace.

To see that is to see his salvation. To see that is to depart in peace. To see that is to walk through life with a steady step and confident heart and a singing spirit. God has come to share my place and in the power of that coming, someday I shall share God's. Here in the manger in Bethlehem is the goal, the hope, the purpose of my life. Here cradled in the straw is the power to become what God wants me to be. Alleluia. O come, let us adore Him, Christ the Lord.

This Christmas Day, weary with your illusions, sick of your failures, tired of your struggles, O I pray you, stand with Simeon and look into the eyes of that Christmas child. Look and keep on looking till you see there the vision of your life as it can become. Look and keep on looking until you see there the burning love of God shining in your darkness. Then go to your homes, to your jobs, to your families in peace. The Prince of Peace has come. God is with us; henceforth be with God. *Lord, now lettest thou thy servant depart in peace, according to thy word; for mine eyes have seen thy salvation.*

Preached at the North Reformed Church, Newark, New Jersey, December 25, 1949.

19

Christmas II

For God so loved the world, that he gave his only
begotten Son, that whosoever believeth in him should
not perish, but have everlasting life.
    John 3:16

Under our Christmas tree at home, when I was a child, we had a little Nativity scene. Each year it was my job to unpack the figures from their box and arrange them into their familiar pattern. The Virgin and child were always placed in the center, with St. Joseph standing by. I would place the kneeling shepherds around the manger and then, approaching the stable on their camels, the three wise men from the East. Every year it was always the same picture. I can recall that as each Christmas came, I would resolve that in one way or another I was going to change that picture, move the wise men to another side or put the shepherds somewhere else. But every year when I tried it, somehow it never seemed to look right and I finally put the figures exactly where they had been the year before. I often think of that youthful experience because it seems to me a kind of symbol of the way in which most of us keep Christmas. We have in our minds a very definite picture of what Christmas ought to be, the inn at Bethlehem, the heavenly chorus of angels filling the midnight sky, the visit of the shepherds to the manger cradle of the newborn child. Every year at Christmastime, just as I used to unpack those little figures from their box, you and I unpack the traditional actors in the Christmas story and put them through their paces. These are the characters which we have come to associate with Christmas. Often as we have heard their stories before, Christmas would simply not be Christmas if we were not able to hear them over again.

But just there lies the tragedy of it all. We all know and love the Christmas story, every last detail of it. We all know the events which took place almost as well as though we ourselves had been present at them. But what those events mean, what their inner and abiding significance may be, of that we are much less certain. Suppose that I were to ask you, "What happened at Christmas?" I do not doubt that every one of you could tell me the whole chain of events, beginning with the journey to Bethlehem right through the coming of the wise men. But suppose that I were to say to you, "That's not what I mean; I know as well as you what happened outwardly. But tell me, what happened inwardly? What was the significance of all these events which you have been describing?" That's when we begin to stammer and stumble for an answer. And that's why Christmas, in spite of all of its magic and beauty, means so little in permanent effect upon our lives. For most of us, it is a traditional story with traditional figures like those in my Christmas box. And so long as those traditional figures are in their right places at the right time, that's all we care about. But to break through the artifice and find the meaning behind the story, and what is more, to grasp that meaning and make it glow permanently in our lives, ah, there is something which few of us seem able to do! By next Sunday the bright world of Christmas will have faded completely, the figures in the story will have been packed away for another year, and those of you who are here will be living once again in the drab, cold world of 1950.

I wonder whether you have ever stopped to realize that in the Gospel according to St. John there is no Christmas story, no shepherd, no angels, no wise men, no manger. In that gospel, when first you meet Jesus Christ, he is a full grown man of thirty. About his birth, his infancy, his childhood, St. John says not one word. Now at first you may think that this is rather a serious omission. Why does St. John leave out the Christmas story? Didn't he know it? Didn't he think it was important? I think he left it out quite deliberately, and for just the reason that I have been indicating. By leaving it out, he is trying to say something to us. It is as though he were saying this, "Matthew and Luke have told you the beautiful story of what happened at Christmas. But so you will not fasten on that story and think that it is the important thing, I am going to tell you something far more important. I am not going to tell you the story; I am going to tell you what the story means. I am not going to tell you what happened; I am going to interpret what happened. You know already about the baby born on a cold winter's night. I am going to show you the inner meaning of that birth, for you and for all humankind."

For God so loved the world that he gave his only begotten Son, that whosoever believeth in him should not perish but have everlasting life. Take away the tinsel and the ornaments, the choirs, the carols, and the candles, all of the traditional figures that clutter up your Christmas outlook, and this is the living heart of it all. Without this, the figures in your Christmas story are of no more value than the little dolls that I used to put under my Christmas tree. Without this, your Christmas celebration will be so much dead formalism, so much empty ceremony, for it is this that gives it its life. Will you try to break through all of the routine things and find this burning wonder, glowing with the fire of a thousand suns? What does Christmas mean? Candles? Carols? Gifts? Cards? Trees? *God so loved the world.*

That's what made the angels sing, the shepherds run, and the wise men come. And there's power enough in it to make every one of us sing and rejoice, no matter how despondent our hearts or despairing our spirits. It's no false joy, no artificial optimism. It holds for good days and bad, for dark ones as well as bright. The future of this world and everyone in it, your future and mine, as well as that of your loved ones, does not belong where you think it belongs. Especially in times like these, it is so easy to whimper and complain, to grow discouraged and downhearted. We throw up our hands and cry, "What's the use?" The world has been left to darkness and greed, murder and lust, handed over to them, and they are running it. Don't talk to me about peace or joy or goodness, not at a time like this! I don't want to hear about them. They don't belong any more—not in the world in which I am living!

If you have been so much as tempted to think like that in these last few weeks, how you need Christmas! For Christmas is the declaration that that is not so! The devil and all his legions want you to believe that this world belongs to the power of darkness; want you to believe that peace and joy and goodwill have no real place, no real future in it; want you to become discouraged, down-hearted; want you to surrender. The discouragement, the gloom, and the pessimism that have taken possession of human hearts recently are a great tribute to the insidious power that darkness and fear and evil have over us, making us surrender to them, compelling us to believe that they have won everything. But they have not won everything, and what is more they cannot. It is this that Christmas wants to proclaim. The final, absolute power in this world is not darkness, is not fear, is not hate, nor any of the forces that represent them. The final, absolute power in this world, against whose power darkness, hate, and fear will finally be shattered, is a God who loves this world.

How much does God love it? Well, enough so that God was willing to become part of it. That's the way God's love works. Looking down and seeing this world, staggering and reeling, torn with strife and sick with pain, God felt only one impulse, saw only one thing to be done. Love is not content merely to look on from the outside, merely to offer bits of advice, helpful suggestions, an occasionally outstretched hand. Love must come in and share to the full. And since God is love, that is exactly what was done. Our human life with its blasted hopes and its broken dreams, its temptations and its passions, its wasted energies and its misdirected aims, ugly, hateful, mean as it is, God loved it, loved it so much that he came to be part of it. And since he has chosen to become part of our human situation, to invade our human scene, nothing, not even the agony of a cross, can frighten him out of it. *God so loved the world that he gave his only begotten Son.*

If you have not reckoned on that fact, which is the fact of Christmas, you will fall into the trap of hopelessness, discouragement, and despair. Pushing against our lives with tremendous force are darkness and war and hate and all the thousand fears which they carry in their train. How can one frail human spirit like yours or mine possibly withstand such pressure? This is how it can. If on the inside of your life there is the mighty force of the love of God, then all of these things will beat against you and beat in vain. Like the house built upon a rock, your life shall stand. And Christmas says, it is on the inside of life that God has come to work. That's why there was a Christmas. That's why God came as a babe in a manger. So that God would no longer have to work outside of us as a stranger, but could work right in our midst, as one of us. And because of Christmas, no matter how violent the world around us may become, within your heart and mine we can resist, and resist with strength.

For, you see, the fact is that God still loves the world, with every bit as much fervor and power as he did on Christmas. And because God still loves the world, he is still giving himself to become part of it. Do you suppose that God who became one of us, who drew our human breath, walked our human pathways rough, suffered our human pain, and finally on the high hill of Calvary died our human death, could forget the whole thing when it was over? Do you want to believe in a capricious kind of God who once took a fancy to human life but now has forgotten all about it? Of course not; what happened in Bethlehem's stable that first Christmas was but the beginning, and the end is not yet, nor will it be until that light has shined into all the world. For it is all the world that Gods loves with an everlasting love. But while that end we cannot see, yet for you and me it means this. The Love that came down at Christmas to enter human life in Christ our Lord still comes down to enter human life in you or in me. No war can stop that. No dictator can stifle it. No darkness can put it out. I do not know where I may have to walk these next few months, nor do you. It may be a very hard and dark and lonely pathway. But I do know this; God so loved the world that he gave me Christ. And so long as that love is in my life, nothing outside can come in and take it away. I stand against darkness, against fear, against all the horrors of this dark night of the soul. But I do not stand alone, not since Christmas. I stand in the love of God who became human for me that I might become his child.

Without that faith, we should all perish. If in this black hour, it is alone that we have to stand, then no matter how gaily you may celebrate Christmas, it is only a celebration. But if that baby there in the manger is really God's love in human form, if I can believe that and be sure of it, if I can be convinced that God cares that much about the world, then I have something that is really everlasting. Nothing can kill it, nothing can take it away, nothing destroy it. When everything else shall fail, this shall remain. I have it now, in life, in death, in suffering, even in hell—and the child in Bethlehem is its proof. *God so loved the world that he gave his only begotten Son.*

Preached at the North Reformed Church, Newark, New Jersey, December 24, 1950.

20

Christmas III

And it came to pass, as the angels were gone away from them into heaven, the shepherds said...Let us now go even unto Bethlehem.
Luke 2:15

That was the critical moment in the Christmas story. I always think it is too bad, whenever the Christmas gospel is read, that so often we stop before this critical moment is reached. You know the parts that are usually read. Mary brings forth her son, wraps him in swaddling clothes, and lays him in a manger, because there is no room for them in the inn. Then the scene shifts to the plains around Bethlehem where the shepherds are tending their flocks and the midnight sky grows brilliant with the angelic choir who chant their exultant hymn, "Glory to God in the highest and on earth peace, goodwill toward men." And there, more often than not, we stop. It is just enough to complete the lovely picture in our minds. But to stop there is to stop before the crucial moment, the important moment. In one sense, even more important than the angels who filled the midnight sky, more important than the news that they brought and the song that they sang is this question: What happened after the angels had gone away?

You can see the importance, can't you? When the skies grew dark once again and life was just what it had been before, suppose that the shepherds had said one to another, "Wasn't that a wonderful experience? My goodness, wait till I get home and tell my family about this! I tell you, this is a night we won't forget for a long time." Suppose they had said that and then gone on about the business of tending their flocks as usual...as though nothing had happened. I won't say that there would have been no Christmas, but I will ask what good it would have been.

You see, this is always life's critical question. What happens to us when the angels are gone away into heaven? O, I do not mean that any of us has ever had or ever will have a like experience. No one of us has ever heard a chorus of angels breaking the silence of a midnight sky. But all of us have had and will have again great moments of experience. Sometimes they occur within our families; sometimes they happen to us in our work; sometimes they come to us when we are alone with our thoughts; often, I trust, they have come to us in terms of our religious faith. How often have they come to us at Christmas when, more than at any other time of the year, we feel at peace with the world, feel that our human lives on this one day, at least, are what God meant them to be. These are the angels who appear to us in our midnight skies—those moments when we see the light and know what we ought to be and what we want to be.

But angels do not stay in the midnight sky. They go away from us into heaven, even as they did from the shepherds. The drab colors soon return as the light fades; the old occupations, the old routines, the old ways are there requiring our attention. We may for a time be able to cherish the memory of some high and happy hour, but that too quickly fades as we become involved in the ordinary business of living. How quickly the story of our lives comes again and again to this same critical point; the angels go away from us into heaven and what will happen then?

I take it that for all of us, probably, this Christmas will be just another experience. We have planned and worked for the joy and gladness of this day; we have eagerly looked forward to its coming. Most of us never get over the thrill of Christmas that we knew when we were children. We love the carols, the lights, the trees, the gifts, the simple goodness and gladness that fill the human heart everywhere at this blessed season. But how quickly it will have gone. In no time at all, the songs will be stilled, the lights will go out; it will no longer be Christmas, it will just be winter. The angels will go away from us once again into heaven. And what will happen then?

Well, when the angels go, there is still the child. A little baby in a manger is not very exciting compared with a choir of angels, but he stays. No matter how dark or quiet the sky may become, he will be there in Bethlehem. No matter how rough or hard life may grow, he will still be there in Bethlehem. For Bethlehem is the everlasting symbol of God's identification with human life. God is here. God will not leave. Moments of exaltation will be followed by moments of depression, life's skies will change a hundred times, the heaven which was once filled with angels may turn dark and threatening, but of this you can always be sure, just as sure of it when your heart is heavy as when it is glad. God is with us, with you, with me, Emmanuel. Bethlehem is but the sign of an everlasting reality which nothing in life or death can ever shake.

And I have the feeling that at Christmas time there are too many of us who hear the angels but too few of us who see the child, too many of us who are raptured by the glamour of the hour but too few of us who are held in the abiding grasp of its reality. The angels will depart; they must depart. But the child remains, the same yesterday, today, and forever. That is why I can imagine no higher commemoration of this glad night than the bread and the wine of Holy Communion; like Bethlehem, they too are the sign and pledge that he is still Emmanuel, God with us, coming to abide with us never leaving us or forsaking us. On our Christmases, our Good

Fridays, our Easters, this is their message, "Lo, I am with you always."

And so this Christmas Eve I wish for you that when the angels have departed into heaven, when the tree has been taken down and the presents put away, the reality will still be yours so that you may live out another year, with whatever it may bring, in the sure confidence that he who was born this day is here with you every day. That is Christmas at its everlasting best. When the angels depart, let us go even unto Bethlehem.

Preached at the North Reformed Church, Newark, New Jersey, December 24, 1954.

21

Christmas IV

And ye are complete in him.
  Colossians 2:10

We all like to crab about Christmas and, judging from recent outbursts in the papers, no one enjoys crabbing more than ministers. But there is something else about Christmas which surely you must have noticed. Despite all the busyness and weariness, despite all the rushing and hustling, despite all the hurrying and pressing, all of which now lie behind us for another year, we still feel on Christmas that there is something wonderful, something good about human life. We may not feel that way again for a whole year. By next Tuesday the wicked and worrisome world may be staring us in the face with manifold problems. But never mind—today for a while at least, we can forget them. We find it easy to be kind; we find it simple to be confident and trusting. People that we are seldom able to tolerate at other times look a little less difficult. There is, as we should all admit, a magic about Christmas. And not the least of that magic is the fact that it is able to cast a spell over our troubled and tense existence, making it seem calm and good, serene and happy.

Christmas, as one of our poets has said, is the place "where all men are at home."

I say that you must all surely have noticed that. I do not intend to spend any more time this Christmas morning in further description of it. Nor do I want to go in to the discouraging question of why it lasts so short a time, why this Christmas experience of peace and goodwill, which we all know, is such a fragile one, so easily and so quickly broken. There is a question that surely we ought to consider, but not on Christmas morning.

No, the question which I should like to tarry with this Christmas morning is really an analysis of that experience. We all know the experience. Now, let us ask ourselves, what creates the experience? What is there in Christmas that spreads this peace and goodwill in our lives? What is there about Christmas that takes the drab and dark facts of human existence and sets them aglow, however briefly, with radiance and beauty? Why is the stable in Bethlehem, in all of its rude bareness, the place where we are at home, yes, even after almost two thousand years, the place, above all others, where you and I feel that we belong, feel at home as we do nowhere else in life? Why?

For an answer, I call your attention to those words of St. Paul's that I quoted a few moments ago. They were written, of course, in a somewhat different context; it may even be that they were written to persuade the Christians of Colossae of a somewhat different point. But however that may be, they say as well as anything in the New Testament what really happens to us at Christmas. They tell us as simply and as fully as anything in Scripture what Christmas has that makes us feel that we belong, that gives us the experience of life at its highest and best. *And ye are complete in him.*

In Christ we are complete. Human life, human existence, find their fulfillment only in Christ. For it is only in Christ that we discover who we really are. There is the basic fact of Christmas. However dimly we may see it, however imperfectly we may grasp it, however much we may sense it without being able fully to express it, it is this which is the real wonder and glory of this day. The child in the cradle is one whom we never weary in welcoming, one of whose coming we never grow tired, no matter how many Christmases we may have celebrated, because the child in the cradle makes us aware of what our lives are really meant to be. The divine possibilities of every human life are here, not as theories in a book, not as sermons from a pulpit, but as a little baby in our midst. *And ye are complete in him.*

Suppose that we try to analyze it a little further. We all know (in fact the church never ceases to remind us) that we are sinners. I seldom use the word, not because I do not believe it, but because the word "sin" is so limited in our understanding that we think sinners are only people in jail, in the gutter, or in the headlines. Suppose we put it another way. Suppose that we say that all of us are bitterly aware that something is missing in our lives. Almost instinctively we all feel that there should be more for us than there is. There are so many unfulfilled dreams, so many unanswered hopes, so many unachieved ambitions, so many unrealized visions. Life is such a bore. We began reaching for the stars, but look what satisfies us now—a new car, an automatic dryer, a hi-fi. Is this what we were made for? Is this what we were meant to be? Can we be bought off with a few appliances? Will these silence those strange haunting whispers in our hearts? Can these satisfy that aching hunger for significance, for fulfillment, which every one of us knows?

I am not going to spend time this Christmas morning discussing the odd ways in which we try to silence those whispers, the strange ways in which we try to satisfy that hunger. Merely to list the mad variety of things which we do in an effort to escape from ourselves, to find meaning for ourselves, would be to set up the Vanity Fair of human existence in all of its tinsel and folly. But I want to expose the wound so it hurts, so we are all aware of it. I want us to know that in the bottom of the heart of every one of us (I care not how successful the world may reckon us) is this ache that comes from the certainty that we could be something more. There must be more to life than we have found—or is it worth it? There must be more to my personality and yours than the dates of our birth and marriage and the tombstone in the cemetery that tells when we died. If you know yourself at all, then you must know that this feeling of frustrated fulfillment, this awful sense of incompleteness is the most haunting thing in human life. You remember Browning's lines?

> Just when we are safest, there's a sunset touch,
> a fancy from a flower-bell, someone's death ....
> And that's enough for fifty hopes and fears
> as old and new at once as nature's self
> to rap and knock and enter in our soul.

But now it's Christmas. Frustrated, unfulfilled, incomplete, insignificant, knowing that we are missing something but not certain what it is, we come to an older place than Eden and a taller town than Rome—Bethlehem. And there is great peace and satisfaction, great contentment and goodwill in our hearts, if only for a little while. We feel at home. What does this child do to us to make such magic in our lives? How is he able to banish so many things which we have never been able to get free from? How is he able to give so much we have been seeking, but seeking in vain?

Don't you know the answer? Let me put it as baldly as I can. Jesus Christ makes us suddenly realize what we really want to be. He lived in one of the smallest and most backward countries of the world. He never traveled more than a hundred miles from his home. Jesus was nobody; he had nothing. When he died his only possessions were literally the clothes on his back. He never went to college; he never owned a house; he never wrote a book. And yet could you say that at any given point in his life he lacked significance; that at any moment from Bethlehem to Calvary he did not have a sense of purpose and accomplishment? This is what attracts us to the cradle and makes us feel at home. A man who had nothing, as we figure it, had the one thing that we want and want desperately—significance. He felt his life meant something.

Or look at it another way. Jesus Christ had a life that we would consider rugged. Born in a barn, he had to flee as a little baby or be murdered by Herod's henchmen. Though we cannot be sure, the evidence seems to be that Joseph died when Jesus was young; he probably had to work to support his family when he was still in his teens. When he began his public ministry, its success was a very temporary one. He lost followers faster than he could gain them. Of the little company on whom Jesus depended one turned out to be a traitor, another was too cowardly to own that he knew him, and the rest were pretty much zeros. Arrested, dragged through the streets like a common criminal, finally crucified, he could count three women and one man as the total result of his work when he died. A depressing story of defeat and frustration—but find me a single sentence from Jesus' lips to indicate that he felt that way. Everything that he said to his last sentence indicated that he died as he had lived, with an invincible sense of being a conqueror. This is what attracts us to Bethlehem and makes us feel at home. We who have been whipped by life till we slink through it like frightened animals look at Jesus whom nothing could defeat. What would you not give to have that in your living?

Well, I could go on with one illustration after another and all to the same point. The things that life really lacks, the good things, the things that would complete our lives and make them whole—they are here. They came into our world this morning. How beautiful to come to Bethlehem and see human personality in its full dimensions, see its courage and its trust, see its significance and its meaning, see its grace and glory, see its strength and victory. Who was it that said, after some nasty episode, that it made him want to resign from the human race? Well, the world makes us feel that way every day. But here on Christmas we are proud to belong to the human race. For here on Christmas we see its complete possibilities. We feel at home, because here in Jesus Christ is what we really are.

And if you say, "Yes, but that is because in Jesus Christ God came in human life," I can only reply, "Exactly, and the abiding significance of this day is that God wants to come into every human life, yours, yours, mine." The thing that ought to make the heart sing and the spirit rejoice this morning is that this completeness which was in Jesus can be in us also. These divine possibilities are not his alone; he has made them ours. *And ye are complete in him.* He was but the first of what God intends to be an endless line of splendor, men and women of ordinary kind who live every day in the faith that they are the children of the Most High, that they have a Father who will never leave them alone.

For after all, what makes life complete? What gives it the things it lacks, the meaning, the significance, the trust, the victory, which we all want? What indeed but the Spirit of God dwelling in us and controlling us? God was, to be sure, in Jesus Christ perfectly and completely. But God can be in us in every growing measure, moving the limits of our existence out into ever increasing likeness to Christ. This is the best of Christmas, that Christmas was only the beginning, only the first scene as it were in a drama which shall not reach its conclusion till a world has been redeemed and restored.

It will soon be over? No, it will never be over. On Christmas Day in Jesus Christ we see the complete person, the person God wants. But we can see so much more if we will. In March, in September, every day of every year we can see the complete person the person of grace more and more in the incompleteness and brokenness of our own lives. Christ was born today. But you and I can also be born to a new life.

And ye are complete in him.

Preached at the North Reformed Church, Newark, New Jersey, December 25, 1960.

22

Christmas V

For the Son of man came...to give his life . . .
Mark 10:45

Perhaps you think that I have my days mixed up. For those words sound much more like Good Friday than they do like the day before Christmas. When that day comes next April, it will be time enough to think about why Jesus came. Now, after all, we are celebrating the fact that Jesus came. Should we not give ourselves over to the gladness of that celebration, basking in the light of Christmas without any trace of shadows? There does seem to be some deep human need in the way in which we alternate our feasts and our fasts. The joy of Christmas is followed by the deepening gloom of Lent and Passiontide, only to be resumed in the glad triumph of Easter. It almost looks, doesn't it, as though we human beings could take just one mood at a time. We can be happy at Christmas; we can be sad on Good Friday. But to try to combine them into a single day is asking too much. We should be content this morning to say, "For the Son of man came." That's enough to celebrate, isn't it, that there in the manger of Bethlehem a baby is born who is both son of man and son of God? *For the Son of man came.* Why not stop there, rejoice in that coming, and let the rest take its course next spring when the scene has shifted from Bethlehem to Calvary?

Well, I certainly do not want to be a kill-joy at Christmas. But I do want to suggest that if you are troubled, as I am, not by the commercialism of Christmas but by its complete insignificance in the total reality of living, here is a possible reason for that insignificance. We knock ourselves silly during this month of December; we go all-out for Christmas as for no other day in the year. To what other celebration, sacred or secular, do we give so much time, effort, and money as we do to this one? But now I ask you. When all is said and done, what significant things do we have to show for it come, let us say, next January? What are the real results of Christmas in our lives? "Unpaid bills and broken toys" is all that many of us could say. And while there are doubtless many reasons for this feeble and insignificant result from such enormous effort and activity, I suggest that one great reason for us Christians may be our failure to understand the full dimensions of what we are celebrating.

For the Son of man came to give his life. You see, if all we have to celebrate is the fact that the Son of man came, that the baby was born, that really is not very much. But that really is all that Christmas tends to be, a little oasis of light in the midst of a dark and cold winter. He came, but he is no longer here. He lit up our dark sky for a moment, but it soon grew dark again. Bethlehem is miles away and years ago; we do well if we can remember it for a single day once a year. But the moment we go on to ask why he came, to put purpose into his coming, to give dimensions to this birthday, then we begin to connect it with the real world in which we live. Then Christmas is not a little island of tinsel and twinkling lights, but a mighty event which reaches out across the miles and the years to catch hold of our human existence today. Then Christmas is not an annual escape from reality, but a lasting invasion of the bitter reality of our trivial and unhappy lives by the great reality of God's redeeming purpose. *For the Son of man came to give his life.*

He came to give his life. He was born to die. Why? Well, before we attempt to answer that question by looking at the desperate situation of our human need, we must attempt to answer it by looking as best we can at the heart of God himself. The Son of man came to give his life because this is what our God is like. Let me put it this way. Christmas is the beginning of God's final effort to show us what he is really like, to clear away our cruel misunderstandings of him, the crippling caricatures and distortions, which block our living in this world as his children. The hard taskmaster, the vengeful tyrant, the capricious and arbitrary despot, the blind force, the unpredictable fate, these are the pictures of God in which people have believed, by which they have lived.

And they still do by the thousands. Play a game sometime with your neighbor, or better still with yourself. Take a piece of paper and put down the first picture that comes to your mind when you hear the single word, God. In many cases it will be an old man with a white beard keeping records in some heavenly accounting office. In many cases it will be an implacable king on a far away throne protected from the agony of earth by rank on rank of angel hosts. In many cases, I fear, there would be nothing on the paper but an oblong-shaped blur. But in how many instances would the picture of God be a baby born in a stable, a man worn out at the end of day by words of comfort and works of healing, a man dying in lonely agony on a cross for someone else's crime?

But *this is God*, the only true picture of God, the only one he has authorized, the only one he has drawn himself in the living character of a human personality. The Son of man came to give his life because from the beginning to the end God is always giving himself to the undeserving that they may be deserving, to the unlovely that they may be lovely, to the stranger and the orphan that they may become his children. From the first moment in which he created a world that he did not need to that last moment in which he shall restore a world that has deliberately forgotten, ignored, and lost him, the God of the gospel, the God of the Christian creed is a God who gives himself. This is what Christmas is here to say. This is what makes it worth celebrating. Christmas gives us a human photograph of the heart of the Eternal. Breathtaking as the revelation is, the way this baby, this man, will react to the human situation is the way God reacts to it. *The Son of man came to give his life.*

I have time to do nothing more than indicate what a difference that kind of Christmas faith can make to the darkest and coldest day in January. When that day comes, instead of asking, "How am I being punished?" when we have really accepted Christmas we say, "What good thing is God trying to give me, even in this cup of bitterness and sorrow?" Instead of saying, "God, how can I buy you off, how can I make you change your mind?" when we have really accepted Christmas we say, "Give me the grace to find the goodness in my cross." Our whole attitude toward life and its problems is changed when we see what Christmas is all about, see that Christmas gives us the true picture of a God who never stops giving himself to his children, who even in the broken and unhappy bits of experience is giving grace and strength and love. This is what Christmas wants to tell us. And if you and I accept it, believe it, our whole world will change. *For the Son of man came to give his life.*

But now we must consider this as well. The Son of man came to give his life because this is what humanity is like. Every one of us is aware of the startling way in which into this world of selfish elbowing, grasping greed, into the mad stampede of human existence there comes at Christmas this little child who does not even claim a place to be born. Even the newspapers will comment on the way in which Christmas reverses all of our ordinary ways of living, giving us a little sample of another way of life. That's what makes Christmas so lovely; it centers not on getting but in giving; it gives us the chance at least once in the year to think about someone else beside ourselves.

But don't stop there! Don't content yourself with the little sample and then drift back to the old and ordinary kind of life for the next year. For the little sample that we see at Christmas, the child who cannot even claim a place to be born, the man who came to give his life is nothing less than God's announcement that this is what our lives must be all the time, shall be all the time when God's grace transforms and remakes them. When the little baby grows to manhood, when the man dies and rises again, this will have been the purpose in it all—to make it possible for us to be like Jesus Christ. And the real dimension of Christ-likeness, which is the final goal and purpose in Christmas, is *to give his life.*

Locked up within our own self-concern, driven by our grasping greed, made miserable by our failure to be the center of the universe, we are suddenly met at Christmas by one who says that there is no hope unless the whole direction of our living be changed. What are the poisons that destroy our humanity, that give it its sickness? Why, they are the very self-concern, egocentricity, and greed without which we think it impossible to live. My life, my will, my purpose, my ambition. And here is Jesus Christ, even as a baby, to say that only when life is moved off its dead center in these things, and moved out into obligation and concern that spend themselves in others—only then will life find significance, satisfaction, and peace.

To give his life…not merely in the final act of Jesus' sacrificial death, but to give his life every day that he lived, to be spending his store of energy in devoted concern for his brethren, that's why Christ came. He was born to die, to die every day to all the claims of his own position and advantage that he might be alive to the needs of those around him. And there is no other way to significant living, satisfied, peaceful living. Listen to the strident clamor of angry voices this Christmas all shouting, "This is what I want; this is what I am going to have; this is what you're going to give me whether you want to or not." The world was so filled with such voices yesterday you could scarcely hear the carols. But are they happy voices? Would you say that that life, that kind of existence brings contentment and meaning?

We may shrink back from the full implication of Christmas a little frightened by it. It is not easy to go out into the cold winter under holy obligation to give ourselves away. It is not comfortable to feel that someone else has a claim upon us. It diminishes our feeling of individualism to know that we belong to someone else. But what are these losses compared with the infinite gain in knowing that we are what we were meant to be, children of God, by the grace of Jesus Christ living the life of our Father in heaven.

And that is how we can go back to life from Christmas. Because we have seen the child we can know that in heaven above there is a God who does not spare but shares, giving himself without limit for the sake of his children. Because we have seen the child we can know that a life of purpose and peace is possible when we live in the possibilities of Jesus Christ—holy obligation that never seeks to save itself, but spends itself for the other, the neighbor, the enemy.

For who is this child and why has he come?

The Son of man came to give his life.

Preached at the North Reformed Church, Newark, New Jersey, December 24, 1961.

23

Christmas VI

In the beginning was the Word,...
and the Word became flesh and dwelt among us.
    John 1:1, 14

How should we explain Jesus Christ? It's interesting to observe how the authors of the four gospels tried to explain him. Mark begins his explanation with John the Baptist, as if to say that Jesus was the continuation and the crown of what John the Baptist had begun. Matthew begins his gospel with a genealogy that goes back to Abraham, the father of the faithful, the first member of the chosen people of God, implying that to understand Jesus Christ we must see him as the founder of God's new people of which Israel was only the promissory symbol. Luke also begins his gospel with a genealogy, but his extends back beyond Abraham to Adam. Jesus Christ is the second Adam, the first member of a new and restored humanity.

Now obviously none of these cancels the other out. Each one picks up and includes what has been said before in an attempt at further definition. Jesus Christ is the successor to John the Baptist; he is the founder of the new people of God; he is the first example of a new humanity. But when John seeks to find the explanation, he goes far beyond what any of his colleagues have dared to try, far beyond John the Baptist, far beyond Abraham, far beyond Adam. In what can only be conscious imitation of the very opening words of the Old Testament, John goes back before creation to discover an adequate explanation for Jesus Christ. *In the beginning was the Word.*

"In the beginning God created." "In the beginning was the Word." It is obvious, is it not, that in John's thinking Genesis and the gospel are linked together. The implications of that linking are far too great for a few moments at a Christmas celebration. But surely we can focus on this one central affirmation. If Genesis begins with the story of creation, John begins with the *new* creation, for nothing less than that was the intention of God in the life, death, and resurrection of Jesus Christ, the Word made flesh. *In the beginning was the Word.*

I suppose it is an inarticulate feeling for this that accounts for the fact that in long Christian tradition Christmas has always been a feast of the animals. It's almost impossible, even for us twentieth-century sophisticated Christians, to imagine a Christmas scene without them, the oxen, the sheep, the camels. Our earliest childhood memories are filled with the recollection of putting them all carefully in their places, but did we ever ask ourselves what they are doing there? Why clutter up the Christmas picture with this miniature zoo? Why spoil the simple concentration on the babe in the manger with all of these creatures?

Of course, it is impossible to extrapolate them from the story; the sheep were there because the shepherds brought them, the camels because the wise men rode them. The oxen because animals of some sort had to be in that stable. But I don't really think that's how it happened. I think it happened because Christian tradition wanted to symbolize the great insight with which John began his gospel. Christmas is the first night of a new creation. When the Word became flesh and dwelt among us, something was begun which will not stop, which cannot stop with the people of God or with the human race itself; something was begun which cannot stop until this whole created universe from the lowliest animals to the stars in their courses, this whole created universe, is once again filled, as on the day of its birth, filled with nothing but the glory of God. *In the beginning was the Word.* What happened in Bethlehem was the initial event in a story which shall not be finished till the vision seen by another John (or was it the same one?) has come to pass. "I saw a new heaven and a new earth."

With that as our charter, with that as the context in which we have been called into being, how much different our role as Christians, as followers of the Word made flesh, now appears. We are no longer in the ghetto, a frightened little band of helpless folk set in hopeless opposition to a wicked and hostile world. As the first fruits of the new creation, we are part of a world which is being remade into the pattern and image of Jesus Christ. We know the final destination, the ultimate design. They're not guesswork; they're not idle speculation. They have been set since that night when the Creative Word became flesh, that night when the Creative Word was let loose in creation. And since that final destination, that ultimate design have been made clear in Jesus, we can struggle with serenity, do battle in confidence, because we share in the power of God who is making all things new.

I have often thought that in all the Christmas cycle of stories the only person who really knew what the score was was King Herod. Not for him the baby in the manger, the insipidly smiling Virgin, the cooing cherubs, the sleepy animals, to be admired for a while and then back to business as usual—which is our way of keeping Christmas. Herod was far too shrewd to be taken in by that foolishness. Instinctively he realized that unless something were done to stop what had happened in Bethlehem's manger, there would be no more business as usual, not for him or for anybody else, not even for the emperor on his painted throne in Rome itself. Something had happened which could destroy them all, or make them all over to the point that they no longer recognized themselves. So Herod had the right reaction to Christmas; he took the sword, vowing to stop it.

Of course, he failed. But the encouraging thing to me is that we shall fail also. Not that we try to stop Christmas with a sword, but not even our smothering of the Word made flesh with ecclesiastical hugs and religious kisses will be able to stop it. The Word, by whom all things were made, and without whom was not anything made that was made—that Word has become flesh, remaking and remolding a fallen and captive creation until it too becomes an instrument for God's glory. The sheer spiritual energy contained in that manger is more than enough to recreate a universe.

And in that work of recreation you and I have been called to have our tiny share. Surely the table to which we are shortly to come is the significant proclamation of that. For what we shall be doing when we take the bread and share in the cup will be sharing in the recreating power of the Word made flesh, a power that is made perfect in weakness, a power that is strengthened by self-emptying and self-denial. We must never forget that the body which we take was broken and the blood which we receive was shed, but however it comes, this is the power that overcomes and remakes the world.

Do you know the lovely lines that Gabriel speaks to Mary in Wiston Auden's great Christmas poem, "For the Time Being"?

> Hear, child, what I am sent to tell;
> Love wills your dreams to happen, so,
> Love's will on earth may be, through you,
> No longer a pretend, but true.

That's the majesty and the mystery of John's version of Christmas, all of our hopes and dreams are no longer a pretend, but true, because

In the beginning was the Word,…and the Word became flesh and dwelt among us.

Preached at New Brunswick Theological Seminary, New Brunswick, New Jersey, December 16, 1977, and at St. John's Church, Essex, New York, December 25, 1979.

24

Christmas VII

Now in this same district there were shepherds out in the fields, keeping watch through the night over their flock, when suddenly there stood before them an angel of the Lord and the splendor of the Lord shone round them....Be not afraid for behold, I bring you good news of a great joy, which will come to all the people.
      Luke 2:8-10

Whenever I am able to read Luke's nativity story freed from all the mystery and the magic which years of association have brought to it, I am always surprised to notice how few religious types are involved. After all, the story begins with Caesar Augustus, the mighty emperor of Rome, whose only interest in religion was his own self-deification. What is that self-serving potentate doing at the beginning of the Christmas story? We could as well expect to hear Gorbachev singing "Silent Night"! But if Caesar Augustus had not sent out his command for a census, there would have been no birth in Bethlehem. Perhaps it is good for us, in Christmas, 1986, to be reminded that God is able to use the proud actions of princes and potentates for his own purposes. It may comfort us this Christmas to know that God still has that power and is using it now in ways that we cannot begin to fathom.

And then the shepherds. I wish we could destylize them from the pageant-like figures that croon carols to each other in Latin. Shepherds were a rowdy bunch, rough people. The pious despised them because they were pretty careless about their religious duties. They had to be rough and ready because it was their job to protect the flock against marauders of every kind, animal and human. But this despised and socially unacceptable group of men was the first to get the message. It didn't come to the scholars of the law, to the scribes or the Pharisees who spent their time poring and praying over prophecy. It came to an unlikely bunch of men with crude life-styles and bad manners who said their prayers only occasionally. Well, would you expect the angel of the Lord to appear to a bunch of steelworkers in Youngstown, Ohio?

And, of course, the angel's news is positively absurd. The new order of things is here. All that the prophets have spoken about has come to pass. Proof? You want proof? Go to Bethlehem and look for a new born baby boy in a cow stall somewhere in a barn behind a tavern! The new age, the new creation, the new world—it's here. And the proof is a baby in a tavern barn. I've often thought it was a good thing that the shepherds were the first to hear that. Simple souls that they were, they probably didn't have the wit to perceive how silly it sounded. Their curiosity was stimulated. Had the first announcement of Christmas come to the priests and the scholars, they would have had so many questions that it would have taken them at least six months to get to Bethlehem. It's so unlikely! Who in his right mind would expect the sign of God's new age to be a squalling kid in what was close to being a slum?

Well, so I could go on. Apart from Mary and Joseph, who else in the whole nativity story has any religious claim to be there? The startling thing about the world which God invaded at Christmas to begin the restoration of his creation is that it was not the religious world of prophets, priests, and preachers, but the very secular scene of politicians, tavern keepers, and working people. That ought not surprise us because it is fully in agreement with God's purpose, which was not to let the pious inherit the earth, but to take broken, faltering, selfish, scheming human creatures with their brutal societies and transform them into sons and daughters of God living openly in the kingdom—the original intention for humanity.

Replacing the old age with a new one is not the point; every politician promises that. But restoring a ruined creation to its original wonder and beauty, putting a broken humanity back together again until once more it reflects the glory of its maker, for that we must go not to imperial Rome or holy Jerusalem or their modern counterparts; for that we must go to Bethlehem and find the babe wrapped in swaddling clothes, lying in a manger.

Karl Barth has a wonderful passage somewhere in which he points out how appropriate it was that Jesus was with the beasts in the stall, a fitting foreshadowing of the time when he would confront the beast in human nature when our bestiality would nail him to the cross. That's not something to be postponed till next Good Friday. The shadow of the cross falls across Bethlehem's cradle, for as the Heidelberg Catechism reminds us, his whole life was part of his passion, Bethlehem as well as Calvary.

It was a pagan Roman emperor who set the whole train of events into motion; it was a group of the fringe of society that first heard the news; the event took place in a cow stall. That's how God's new creation began. I don't wonder that the shepherds went back glorifying and praising God for all they had heard and seen. We all should; we all should. For the meaning of the story is that God takes the whole world seriously; that God comes to redeem the secular as well as the sacred; that God is just as concerned with College Avenue in this township as, with Old First, this church. And God does it all in his own strange way which sometimes makes us very impatient. Of course Caesar Augustus had no idea about the baby born in Bethlehem, but who could have imagined that in a few short centuries that baby would have pushed the great imperial throne into oblivion? And who needs to be reminded that that same power of Bethlehem is still at work in the secular world of computers, multinationals, and superpowers of 1986? We all do; we all do. And that's what makes Christmas merry!

Did you ever wonder who the gentlemen are in that old carol, "God Rest Ye Merry, Gentlemen"? They are not saints or scholars, preachers or priests; they are simply ordinary folk, people of the world of Albany, Rensselaer, or Greene County. But they as well as we can remain merry, our God will keep them merry, because Christ has been born into the world of ordinary men and women. Because of the baby born this night in Bethlehem's manger, our whole world is safe, safe because it is loved by nothing less than the great heart of God. Friends, God rest you merry; the Lord has come!

Preached at Bethany Community Church (Reformed), Albany, New York, December 24, 1986.

Part IV

Easter Sunday

25

Easter Sunday I

Jesus saith unto her, Mary. She turned herself, and
saith unto him Rabboni; which is to say, Master.
    John 20:16

These simple words recount in very truth the greatest turning point in history. For here, in its very simplest terms, is set forth that living encounter which is the real foundation on which is built all of the joy and gladness of Easter Day. Mary Magdalene making her sorrowful, halting journey to the tomb of Christ that first Easter morning is but a symbol of you and me in the bewilderment and loneliness of our lives. The few things in life that had held meaning for her, centered as they were in the personality of Jesus, had all been swept away and she had been cast out alone into a heartless and careless world, with not so much as a body in a grave to serve as a memorial of the days of happiness and contentment which she had once known. "They have taken away my Lord and I know not where they have laid him." That was the attitude, the outlook upon life which she had in the garden that morning. There was no hope, no joy, no sense of belonging or being at rest; there was only a vast unknown all about her, with no more friendly hand, no more reassuring voice, no more steadying eye. Mary Magdalene never realized with the bitter intensity that she did that morning how utterly desolate and alone she had been left, with no meaning in the life that she knew, and no hope of anything better to come in the days that lay before her.

And then, it happened. In that garden, in the cool of the Easter dawn, something happened which changed all that, which swept it all away. That garden was the scene of a living encounter, a grand encounter which made of Mary Magdalene a new person, with a completely different attitude and outlook upon life, with joy and hope singing in her heart. Through the gray mists of the dawn, she heard one calling her by name, one who knew her, one who yet cared for her. "Mary." And to the call of that voice and the living person who called she had but one response—to answer out of the fullness of her heart, "Rabboni, My Lord and My Master."

Easter has meaning only because down through the long centuries since that first encounter, men and women have kept coming to this same garden of broken dreams and lost hopes there to meet with the same experience. Sometimes you and I have come there in the loneliness and desolateness of hearts that the world has beaten and defeated; lives that no longer have any hope or any purpose. We have lost all desire to go on living, nothing means anything anymore, the troubles and trials of life have been too much for us. Flattering words, fine programs, high-sounding promises—life is full of these; they are to be had for little or nothing almost any place we care to buy them. But let them all vanish into the thin air of which they are made, let the human heart be so gorged with them that it cannot stomach them any longer, and what is there left? Is the world any less ruthless, is human society any the better for them? Is life in the specific places in which you and I have to live it any the easier because of these cheap platitudes and easy slogans of comfort? Do they ease its burden, comfort the aching wounds of the heart, make the toiling and the sweating any the less difficult? Ah, the bitter truth is that many of us come to this Easter garden so disillusioned by all that we have been told that we have collapsed in the face of life and have not the heart to go on. Where is the peace that was promised us when the clouds of war should be driven away? Where is the new world that was to come out of the struggle and agony of our time? Can men and women like us go on for endless generations of struggle and fear, of trust in military might and selfish power, can we spend our lives in an armed camp, can we go on building homes and raising families, not knowing what may happen to them in a month or a year? Life is crowding in to conquer us, to prove to be too much for us; the old familiar landmarks are gone and we are left alone, defeated and afraid.

Ah, with what a thrill to the heart comes the grand encounter of Easter when life has left us like that! Just when there seems to be nothing left, when everything seems to have been swept away in the confusion, there comes that voice with an unmistakable clarity, calling us by name. We turn and behold the living Lord and Master, the one that we had thought dead, the one that we had written off as of no importance, the one whom everybody thought had been defeated and sent to his death, banished from the life of the world. There he stands, alive, victorious. They thought they had him defeated, but they forgot to reckon on the power that was behind him. They thought they had him out of the way, but they didn't know that a grave meant nothing to Jesus. They thought that they had finished with him once and for all, but they overlooked the fact that God was in the struggle and always has the last word. And, don't you see, when that grand encounter takes place, when in the Easter garden, with minds filled with tragedy, defeat, and bitterness, vividly recalling the agony and the horror and the blood of Good Friday, when there we meet the living Lord, when there he calls you by name and you answer, my master, don't you see, something has happened there, something has happened to your life and mine to change them down to the very depths of their being? Defeat, Tragedy, Loneliness—name them off as you will—here is one who has met them all and still lives. And what is more, in this victorious life, Jesus has met you, called you by name. He will be the new factor in your life, his life which nothing could defeat or break will be added to yours. In his communion and comradeship, you and I can scorn all of the defeats and tragedies of life—what do they amount to? Here is the power that is marching on to victory, the power that nothing can stop, the power of God in the risen Lord of Easter. That power has met you in a living encounter, claimed you for his own, and, gathering you up to himself, takes you on to a triumph which none can take away from you. *Jesus saith into her, Mary. She turned herself and saith unto him, Rabboni.*

But perhaps you and I have come to this Easter garden with hearts that ache and are heavy from a sorrow that nothing can seem to heal. There have fallen on our ears those words, "Earth to earth, ashes to ashes, and dust to dust." Could anything be more final than that? Could anything be more terribly disheartening, more bitterly disillusioning? O the love that we lavished upon them, the joy that we had with them, the hope and the promise that they had in their lives—and here it all ends, in gray dust and ashes! There is nothing that can quite take the heart out of us like this—to follow in thought and love one on whose face we can never look again. Nothing can cast quite such a pall over life, cast it over with chilling fears and numbing sorrows. Like Mary Magdalene, with vacant and lonely hearts, we look sadly after them, "They have taken him away and I know not where they have laid him." There is scarcely one of us who has not felt this chilling finger laid upon our hearts, scarcely one who does not come into the Easter garden with sorrow like that.

And once again, in this thrilling encounter of Easter day, what a magnificent assurance there is for hearts that are heavy with that sorrow! You and I do not come here to celebrate old memories, the influence of a life that lives on in our minds, the Christ idea, the Christ principle, or anything of the sort. You and I come here to be met by a living person, with the reality and the assurance that living personality has. Death was not enough to keep Jesus down; could not snatch him away from us forever. And surely, if the power of love was great enough to carry him through death's swelling wave safely, then there is hope for you and for me and for those we love, hope and assurance that a handful of gray ashes is not the end, that the disillusioned bitter loneliness of life is not its final meaning, hope and assurance that this sacred and precious thing which we know as human personality is not shattered by the shock of death but goes on in newer and larger worlds of peace and joy and light.

But that hope, that assurance for which all of our hearts long so desperately cannot be had just by wishing for it, cannot be had by trying to hide the grim facts of death with paper flowers and canary birds. You and I will not find it in ourselves or in any of our speculations, psychic experiments, or vapid theorizings. Here is where you find it, as in the Easter garden you and I come into living encounter with this master of death, hear him call us by name, hear him call those that we have loved by name, and fall down with the adoring cry, "Master" upon our lips. Out of that meeting, out of that interaction of person with person, out of that grand encounter there springs the calm assurance that Jesus' grasp of love can carry us even across the cold wave of death, that he who was willing to brave even the last agony for us has not brought back any empty victory, any self-sin spoils, but that he will share them with us as we meet him in this encounter of heart with heart. The life that can beat down even death itself is born in this living encounter with Jesus who himself vanquished death, and upon our keeping that comradeship alive and vibrant and real by the power of a living faith. *Jesus saith unto her, Mary. She turned herself and saith unto him, Rabboni.*

Here you and I touch the very heart of the mystery and the reality of our blessed faith! We do such perverse and even stupid things with this religion of ours. We try to make it a moral code, a set of rules and regulations; well, what kind of reality and life does a moral code possess? We try to make it a set of ideas and theories; but what good are they in the places in which we have to travel, who cares about them? If Easter does nothing else for you and me, God grant that it may at least give us to see this much; that the very heart of our Christian faith is a living encounter between living personalities, you and I coming face to face with the risen and living Lord even as did Mary of Magdala by the empty tomb. This is the thing that makes Christianity sparkle and shine with wonder and beauty far above all the other faiths of the world—that at its heart there stands not a code of laws, not a set of ideas, but a living all-powerful person who can become the comrade of your journey and mine, with whom you and I can speak as friend with friend, whose mind we may learn, whose will we can follow, and on whose inexhaustible store of love we may forever draw—yes, to whom we can look even in the last great agony of life to gather us up and bear us through even to his Father's house.

That is the one that you and I must meet with this Easter morning. For Easter is a confrontation, Easter is a grand encounter. Into the desolate wastes of our lives, in the lonely wilderness of our hearts, into the sorrowful pathways of our spirits, Jesus comes, calling you and me by name. We have wandered far, down many a useless pathway, chased many an empty shadow thinking that it was reality. We have tried to banish him from our lives, tried to reduce him to the statues of useless decoration, filled up our hearts with all other kinds of interests and delights, but no matter. The living, risen Lord of Easter, whom death could not hold and hatred and bitterness could not defeat, stands before you and me this morning in this grand and living encounter. And with him he brings the gift of life— life that can be scourged and buffeted, despised and hated, wounded, and even killed—but yet never extinguished, never driven off the field. In the dawn of this his new day, he calls to you and me. Is this the kind of victory that you would like to have in your life; is this the kind of hope that you hold for those that you have loved; is this the kind of foundation on which you would like your life to be built, your heart anchored? Then in this Easter confrontation, gaze up into those strong undefeated eyes and cry with Mary Magdalene, "Rabboni my Master."

Some of you may know those lines of Matthew Arnold, written out of that desolation and bitterness of spirit which so intimately reflects the mood of the world in which you and I live.

> Now he is dead, far hence he lies
> In the lorn Syrian town;
> And on His grave with shining eyes
> The Syrian stars look down.

Is that the faith that nerves and strengthens you and me this Easter day—not the faith we profess merely, but the faith by which we live? Is that all that we have—a Christ that lies dead far hence in some Syrian town? Well, until you and I have met Jesus alive in the grand Easter encounter, it might as well be. Unless you and I know him, meet him face to face, look to him and love him, it might as well be.

But the real message of Easter is a far different one. One of the dramas of these solemn days tells how the soldier who had nailed our Lord to his cross comes back to report to Pilate on his assignment. When he has finished his gruesome story, the wife of Pilate asks, "Do you really think he's dead, then?" "No, I don't," is his prompt reply. "But, where is he?" "Let loose into all the world where neither Roman nor Jew can stop him!"

And so it is. Christ, the living Lord, has been let loose into all the world and in century after century and place after place, he has met men and women in this living encounter, calling them by name, laying his strong hand upon them, making himself their living Lord, their eternal companion, their never failing friend. Amidst all the bewilderment, the confusion, and the sorrow of life, they have heard his voice calling them, have turned to bow before him as Master and as Lord—and out of that encounter with Jesus there has been born in their hearts a joy, a hope, and a life that could not be broken because they were his. This is the grand encounter of Easter—the living Christ and you and I met together in bonds which nothing can break. *Jesus saith unto her, Mary. She turned herself and saith unto him, Master.*

Preached at the North Reformed Church, Newark, New Jersey, April 21, 1946.

26

Easter Sunday II

God hath made that same Jesus, whom ye
have crucified, both Lord and Christ.
　　Acts 2:36

It is not difficult in days like these in which we live to feel that
there is something a bit artificial, something a little forced about
Easter. It bursts upon the winter of our lives with an optimism that
the facts scarcely seem to warrant. To be sure, it has a certain
appropriateness in the springtime when the flowers pushing up
through the earth and the buds opening on the trees testify to the
ever-recurring pattern of life after death. Evidently there is a certain
harmony between the celebration of Easter and the cycle nature
follows; apparently there is in the Easter festival a certain symbolism
of what does in fact happen in the changing of the seasons. But it
becomes rather dangerous, doesn't it, when we try to apply the law
any further than that. To move the Easter rhythm of life after death
out and apply it to our human life and to our human situation is all
too often to yield to a crude and unthinking optimism in which
times like these will not permit us to indulge. You know all the
things which we commonly say that Easter means, that good
triumphs over bad, that life triumphs over death, that gladness

triumphs over sorrow. We like to think that, automatically, human life just works that way. But does it? It certainly is a cheery and comforting way to look at life, but do you really think it is true?

You see, this is our problem at Easter, to make the festival fit the facts, to make Easter something more than a castle in the air, something more than pretty land of make-believe where the story always ends happily. And how much of the routine celebrating that we do belongs quite simply in that category. How a stranger would laugh at us this morning. Here we are thronging to celebrate the victory of life over death, of joy over sadness, of love over hate and all the rest of it—and tomorrow most of us will go back to pick life up just where we left it, with its defeats, its sorrows, its hatreds, and its death, exactly as though nothing had happened. This is what I mean when I say that Easter is for too many of us a pretty world of make-believe, a forced and artificial celebration of an experience in which all of us would like to believe, but in which, in point of fact, all too few of us have ever shared. Can we make it anything else this morning?

We can; but we shall have to go back and start with Good Friday. For Good Friday and Easter, as someone has said, belong together like the dark and the light of the moon. We can never bring Easter into reality; it must always remain a never-never land of make believe, so long as we continue to think of Easter as something automatic and inevitable in the cycle of things. We shall bring Easter into reality, make the festival fit the facts, only when we put Easter where it belongs, with Good Friday. For Easter is the other side of the cross. This is the thing that stands behind these words of St. Peter taken from his first sermon. *God hath made that same Jesus, whom ye have crucified, both Lord and Christ.* See, you cannot pull Easter and Good Friday apart. This same Jesus that you crucified, not some fairy prince, not some spirit hovering in thin air, not some lily bud always blossoming in the springtime, not some noble idea or lofty principle, but this same flesh and blood human being into whose hands you drove the nails and into whose side you thrust the spear, this same man who hung in shame and agony on Calvary and who died in blood upon its cross—this same man and no other God hath made Lord and Christ. Easter is the other side of the cross!

To begin to understand what this means, to begin to comprehend what Easter is, you and I have to recognize that the world in which we live, the little world of our own individual living as well as the great pattern of international living, is still the world of the Sanhedrin, of Pilate, of Judas, of the mob. The picture has not changed in one single detail. Success is still a sufficient reason for any action; self-will is still the chief motive of individuals and of nations; force is still thought to be the best guarantee of truth. Do not think of Pilate and Judas and Caiaphas and all the other actors of Calvary's dire drama as period pieces from a remote time and place. They would be very much at home in the world in which we live, for it is a world which still tries to live by the same old rules. In short, when St. Peter speaks of this same Jesus whom you have crucified, he is not speaking merely to the people of the Jerusalem of two thousand years ago; he is accusing every person present in this church this Easter morning. For each one of us in his own living has played with the very things which brought Jesus to the cross.

But more than that; these games of pride and self-deception and stubborn willfulness which we play with ourselves and with each other while the son of man hangs on Calvary are the things that destroy and ruin and tear our own lives. The world today is groaning in darkness because we all from the least to the greatest insist upon playing out our lives in this fashion and on these terms. The suffering and the sadness, the anguish and anxiety of soul that even the most careless of us has been made to know in these days—they are but the products of the same old sins, the same old follies that once nailed our Lord to his cross. Indeed, if you care to put it that way, he is still on his cross, kept there by our repetition in our time and in our way of the lying and the deceit, the evasiveness and the selfishness and all the other things that once moved the heart of Pilate or Caiaphas. We speak of Peter's denying him thrice; but who of us has not denied him many times over? We shake our heads at Judas' betrayal, but how many times have we betrayed him shamelessly in our lives? We condemn Pilate's refusal of responsibility for him, and then time and again we refuse to take any responsibility for him in the most elementary decisions of our lives.

And so our world is on Calvary. Why blink the facts? Life is sick; poisoned at its source. Powers which can mean only destruction are in the saddle and they seem to be riding high, wide, and handsome to the finish. Force is the king; sheer naked power is the only thing that can command respect; propaganda has replaced truth; justice has been dethroned by expediency; struggle is the watchword of the day. This is the kind of world in which we live. What can we do but come to terms with it, find a way to get along with it somehow? The time is past when we can soothe ourselves with Sunday syrup and beautiful stories. This is the way the world is and we are sick to death of it, but who can stop it? Our hearts are bowed down under the tyranny of such masters, our spirits are sick with the horror of them, our minds are frightened by the prospect of them, but why pretend? Life has come to be like that and what can you do about it but yield? And with life like that we come to the celebration of Easter?

This same Jesus whom ye have crucified God hath made both Lord and Christ. Ah, thank God for the other side of the cross! Easter a fairy tale, a make-believe world? Not at all; it's the one solid thing that you and I have left in life! You say we live in a world in which goodness and decency, goodwill and kindness, justice and peace are being ruthlessly trampled under foot by hatred and power and greed? What can we do? Where can we turn? Why turn to Easter! *That same Jesus whom ye have crucified God hath made both Lord and Christ!* Walter Hampden, that great Shakespearean actor, was once asked what he considered the greatest sentence in the English language. His questioner expected some famous line of Shakespeare in reply, but to his utter amazement the actor answered with a verse from a Negro spiritual, "Nobody knows the trouble I've seen, Glory Hallelujah."

That's it; there's the heart of it. This is what Easter says to you and me. Justice and decency and peace and happiness and all the things you hold dear may go down time and again before the power of hate and pride and force. And you may think it is all over with them. But don't believe it, don't believe it. They went down once in an agony of blood on Calvary when Jesus Christ bowed his head and died, but God won't let it stop there! For God takes the very one whom the world has rejected and puts life and power into his hands. Hatred and force and pride and greed in control of our world? Nonsense; God is in command and when the world has finished and buried its Christ in a tomb, God rolls away the stone and brings him forth with all power given unto him.

How do I know that force and power are weak and ineffectual things which are full of sound and fury but mean nothing? Because Christ has risen. They hurled the full fury of their strength against him; they mocked him, they dragged him to the cross and nailed him there, and then they were through; they could accomplish nothing more. And when on Easter he came back as Lord and Christ, their strength was gone and he was master. And so when I see them today playing the same old game and the world running after them, I am not alarmed, because I know that Christ is risen and therefore the real power and the real force are in the nail-pierced hands of him whom they thought they had killed, because God has made him Lord and Christ!

And how do I know that hatred is a puny thing which is not even worthy of notice? Because Christ is risen. O hatred had its day there on Calvary; it jeered and it mocked and spat out its black venom, never stopping until he breathed his last; and then it was through; it could do nothing more. But God was not through, and when Jesus burst forth from the tomb on Easter, hatred was powerless to touch him. And so today when I hear the lying and the deceit and the stirring up of conflict and bitterness and see people everywhere eager to hear it, I am not deceived, for I know that Christ is risen and that hatred has been defeated once and for all by the power of his love Who could forgive even from the cross, because God has made him Lord and Christ!

Yes, and how do I know that death is a bogeyman who puts on a mask to frighten us but is in fact a weakling? Because Christ is risen. Death certainly had its full chance there on Good Friday. It claimed the life of the son of God, snuffed out in black night the only light the world had ever had; and then it was through; it had done the worst that it knew how. But when on Easter he walked again in the garden, where was death then? Master? No. Jesus was Master whom death could not hold. And so when I must needs walk in the valley of the shadow and part company for a time with one that I have loved, I may sorrow, because I am human, but I am not afraid, for I know that Christ is risen and that death has lost its sting once and for all by the power of him who came that we might have life and have it more abundantly, because God had made him Lord and Christ!

That's the faith of Easter. The cross is there, but there is always the other side of the cross. Nobody knows the trouble I've seen, yes, there is bound to be trouble, sorrow, suffering, so long as the world lives in the spell of its sin and does away with the only one who can save it. But Glory Hallelujah! He is risen. God hath made him Lord and Christ and he shall reign forever and ever. The powers of darkness and death that haunt our world are not in command, not in control. They cannot frighten us or alarm us or cause us to lose hope and surrender. He is in control, for he is risen, risen from the death to which they sought to bring him. And because of that great unshakable fact, you and I can be sure that even in the destruction and tumult of our calamitous days he will rise, for God hath made that same Jesus whom they have crucified both Lord and Christ!

Does your life know that strength and that hope? Unless it does, what good is Easter? But if it does, then you know that in him, nothing can stop you from victory. All the suffering, all the sadness, all the fear and anxiety that life brings to you are but the shadow of the cross. And all the joys and all the blessings, all the hope and all the gladness which life brings to you are but the reflection of his resurrection. How desperately we need that faith and that hope today. Darkness everywhere, fear in every heart, anxiety in every soul, life surrounded by the old powers of death and hell on every side. It certainly looks like a cross, doesn't it? Ought we not surrender, admit that they have won, give our lives over to them? Ah no—there is the other side of the cross. Christ is risen; the battle is not in vain, hope is not empty, faith is not useless. *For God hath made that same Jesus, whom ye have crucified, both Lord and Christ* and into his hands you can entrust your life and know that the victory is certain.

Preached at the North Reformed Church, Newark, New Jersey, March 28, 1948.

27

Easter Sunday III

*Then said Jesus unto them, Be not afraid: go tell my
brethren that they go into Galilee, and there shall they
see me.*
    Matthew 28:10

But we are afraid! Even on Easter morning we are afraid! Or
rather, Easter is at best a kind of temporary distraction from our
fear. It succeeds for an hour or so in taking our minds off our
problems, in diverting our attention from our difficulties and our
trials. For a little while the beauty of the morning, the clean smell
of spring, the festive gladness catch our hearts up in exaltation,
make us forget our fears. But Easter does not last forever; it is only
one day. And even before the sun sets on the day, the grip of the
glory begins to relax and we feel ourselves let down once again into
the world of fear and frustration. O, it is good to have Easters dotted
around in our calendars, good to have these high points of glory that
can occasionally lift us above life's mists and its gloom. But after we
have climbed to the peak, we know perfectly well that the descent
must begin once again that will take us back into the land of
shadows and darkness and death. That is our Easter experience—
a fleeting hour of transfigured glory, followed by days and weeks
and months of life as it always has been.

So it is true this Easter that though with the top of our minds we may be glad and exultant, our deepest fears and our lasting doubts are still there underneath, waiting to receive us again when the excitement has subsided and we have come back to normal. You sometimes wonder how it is that you can come to church on Easter Day, hear the thrilling Easter gospel, sing the glorious Easter hymns, be lifted up so high by the majestic wonder of the occasion, and really believe it all only to be let down so quickly and so completely back to the old level of life, as though you had never been up there on the mountain peak. "Be not afraid," says our Lord. "Be not afraid," sing the hymns. "Be not afraid," says the gospel. "Be not afraid," says the preacher. And we know we should not be. We don't want to be. Who of us would choose to be ravaged by fear and haunted by terror if we really thought it possible to be quit of them once and for all, to stand forth in life free from their dire and dread power? Not one of us. Who wants to be afraid? And yet, despite the voice of Christ, the church, and the gospel crying to us this Easter day, "Be not afraid," we know that next week we shall be, that we shall be caught in that terrible dilemma in which each one of us stands, afraid to go on living because we shrink from its prospects, and afraid to die because we do not know what lies in store for us there either.

Indeed, I think of the two fears, the fear of life is the worse. Most of us are not afraid of death. In my ministry, I have seen precious few people who were really afraid to die. There is about death the air of mystery and adventure that stimulates our curiosity. We may be afraid to have our loved ones die, but we are not afraid to die ourselves. But afraid to live, ah, that's a different question! To face the prospect of what this world may be like in three or five years; to think what may happen to our homes, to our standard of living, to our families, to our security; to watch the steady disintegration of all that we have held dear, the slow destruction of everything we thought important; to stand by while one thing after another is picked out from underneath us until there seems to be nothing left on which we can stand—can any of us face that and not be afraid? Ah, for what life is doing to us in these days, Easter with its brief hour of artificial glory seems a poor tonic indeed! *Be not afraid!* We *are* afraid, and one Easter service a year is not going to change it!

Now that that is true of every one of us, nobody, I dare say, can deny. But I must point out to you that there has been in the world's history at least one group of people of whom it was not true, one group of men and women who on an Easter morning lost their fears and lost them once and for all. It is just stubborn historical fact that once they crossed the dividing line of an Easter morning, never again were they afraid to live, and certainly never were they afraid to die. That group of people was the disciples. I hesitate to name them because we romanticize them so. We conjure up visions of patriarchal men with long beards and flowing robes, women in the dress of the Middle East, all going through prescribed religious motions, and we label them "disciples." But the fact is that they were very real, very human, very ordinary people. None of them was as well educated as you are, and the poorest of you sees more money in a month than they saw in a year.

And they were afraid, just as afraid of life as you. They were pawns in the hands of an imperial despotism that would as soon crush out your life as look at you. They had no security. Their homes might be destroyed at a moment's notice, their young men taken and sold into slavery. Some cheat of a tax collector would probably swindle them out of the little bit they had managed to save. And in addition to all the thousand shocks and fears that life in those days was heir to, these people had staked everything on the success of a man who had turned out to be a complete failure. Jesus was gone, and with him, three of the best years of their lives had gone too, leaving nothing but bitter memories. How silly they looked, they who a few short months ago had dreamed of sitting with him on a palace throne! Now it was just a toss-up whether the same combination of religious and imperial authority that had closed in on him might not close in on them too. They had nothing to look forward to on Saturday night.

But will you look at them on Monday morning? This is a man named Peter who last week tried to claim that he had never even seen Jesus Christ. Look at him now! There he is speaking to thousands of people under the noses of men who he knows would like to kill him. He is not afraid? What has happened? And this is a man named John who last Friday stood wringing his hands wondering what he could salvage out of the wreck of his life. Look at him now, even amid the crashing of empires and the fury of the killing time, saying Alleluia, For The Lord God Omnipotent Reigneth. He's not afraid! What has happened to him? And here is Thomas, that cynical fatalist, who thought it better to die with the cause than live and be made a fool of, going clear to the Ganges River in India to preach the gospel of a man whom in life he had never really trusted. He's not afraid! I care not what you think happened on Easter, fairytale, myth, or whatever. I simply introduce to you Peter, John, and Thomas as they were on Saturday and as they are on Monday and challenge you to deny that something tremendous happened in between!

Then let me introduce you to Sam Jones, and Howard Hageman, and Mary Smith, let me introduce you to ourselves, poor crawling creatures, with a sinking feeling in the pit of our stomachs when we pick up the morning paper, afraid of life, afraid of death. This is the way we were on Saturday; this is the way we shall be on Monday, Easter or no Easter in between. Don't tell me the disciples were more heroic than you are; they weren't. They were just as silly, stupid, and selfish as you—or I. Don't tell me that the record has been pointed up and decorated to make it more impressive. It has not been. The transformation wrought in their lives is imbedded in history so deeply that nobody could change it. Don't tell me that theirs was a religious age while ours is not. The astrologers, the spiritualists, the soothsayers make just as much money today as they did then, if not more. Then why could that one day take fear out of their lives once and for all and leave it still spreading its ugly poisons through yours and mine? To them *be not afraid* became flesh and bone of their living. To us, it is only a religious sentiment. Why?

"Go tell my brethren to go into Galilee, and there shall they see me." That is what our Lord said to those women, directly after he had said, "Be not afraid." I think we slide over those words as a mere detail of geography. Stop with them for a minute. They are very important. Remember, John and Peter and Tom had not seen him yet. So far as they knew, he was still moldering in the grave. Nor would they see him, except in Galilee. Now why Galilee? Why not there in the garden of power and victory? Why not there in the place of beauty and glory? Why in Galilee? Because Galilee was their home, the place where they lived and worked, the home of their families and their friends. In other words, Galilee was the ordinary, every-day situation of their lives. An insignificant little lake country, peopled by humble folk in their towns and villages, it was nevertheless the place of their homes, their work, their association. *Go into Galilee, and there shall they see me!*

Now I wonder … could this be the clue to our problem? For is it not true that for us Easter is something that happens in churches while the bells peal out and the choirs sing and the lilies wave? We can think easily enough of Easter in the North Church, Easter up on Eagle Rock as the dawn reddens the sky, Easter on a morn of beauty that is aglow with soft springtime wonder. That's fine! But Easter in your kitchen? Easter in your office? Easter in your factory? Easter in your home life? Easter in Korea? Easter in a sickroom? The two things don't belong together, you say. Ah, but they do! Don't you see, these are your Galilees. These are the places where you will see Jesus. These are the places where you must see Jesus, if you are not to be afraid.

Every year we build an Easter garden, sing our hymns, chant our glad Alleluias. "Christ is risen!" we say. Then we go back to our homes, back to our jobs, back to our schools, exactly as though he were not. For all you could tell from our lives, he is lying in some lone Syrian grave. If Jesus should come into your house tomorrow night while you were having supper, as once he did when his disciples were eating together, you wouldn't know what to do! If, while you were busy with your job, suddenly you should see him along side of you next Tuesday, as Peter and John once did, you would jump out of your skin. But that is where you should expect him—not in some artificial, decorative garden that has no connection with life. You will not see him there. You have not experienced the living Christ, you don't have a baby's idea of what Easter is all about, until you have met him in the common, ordinary routine business of living and dying in the little place where you are. That's the Galilee where you shall see him ... Jesus, mark you, not the gaudily decked Easter bunny that we try to make him when we parade around in our spring finery, but the all-powerful, stern-eyed conqueror of hell and death who meets us in the hell and death of our own lives.

Be not afraid. Why, when you have met Jesus in Galilee, how can you be afraid? If you have met him only in the garden, only met the figure in a stained-glass window, of course on Monday morning you will crumple like a house of cards when life hits you. But if you have met him in Galilee, ah, then it is a different story! In the Galilee of temptation, you meet him who was himself tempted in all points but resisted and lives to strengthen you to resist also. *Be not afraid.* In the Galilee of hatred, you meet him who was hated and hounded to the death, but who always loved and lives to help you love also. *Be not afraid.* In the Galilee of loneliness, you meet him who was despised and rejected but was yet so close to God that he never felt alone, and who lives to bring you that close to God too. *Be not afraid.* In the Galilee of war and rumour of war, you meet him who with the sole weapon of a cross has brought all the proud empires of this world into ruin and lives to fashion a new empire of love which shall not be defeated, no matter how we may try to thwart it. *Be not afraid.* In the Galilee of pain, you meet him who bore in his body the pain of the cross and in his heart the greater pain of human sin, yet not unto bitterness, but unto love, who lives to help you redeem your pain. *Be not afraid.* In the Galilee of death, you meet him who was himself dead and buried, but who proved that the life of God can break even the finality of death, and he lives to prove it again and again in the lives of his own. *Be not afraid.*

My friends, it is a frightening world in which we live, and it is not likely to become less so. If Christ be not risen, then we have nothing to do but wait until the darkness has swallowed us all up. But Christ is risen! And you need not be afraid. I can tell you that, and you will not believe it. We can paint and picture it here in a thousand different ways, and you still will not believe it. Go back to your homes, to your jobs, to your lives, expecting them to be different tomorrow morning, expecting to find in them the power and the presence of the risen Christ. And you will find him, waiting for you in Galilee, in the place where you live. And having found him, you will find the end of your fears. For Jesus says to you this Easter day, *Be not afraid, go tell my brethren to go to Galilee—there shall they see me.*

Preached at the North Reformed Church, Newark, New Jersey, March 25, 1951.

28

Easter Sunday IV

*I am the resurrection, and the life: he that believeth
in me, though he were dead, yet shall he live: And
whosoever liveth and believeth in me shall never die.
Believest thou this?*
John 11:25-26

Believest thou this? And the most truthful answer, I suppose, is
that we do not! O, don't misunderstand me; it's not that we don't
have some faith in the thing that our Lord is talking about.
Obviously we do, or we would not be here this morning. Much as
we jest about Easter congregations, it takes more than the mere
persistence of blind social custom to account for them, doesn't it?
There is something in the Easter gospel that still tugs at our
heartstrings, that still can pull our unwilling feet to church, no
matter how seldom they may carry us there the rest of the year. We
are not entirely without faith in the thing of which our Lord was
speaking. I knew a family once who had inherited a grand piano.
There it sat in the living room, carefully polished and regularly
tuned. But no one in the house knew how to play it, except one
member of the family who could, if called on, thump out a passable
version of "My Country, 'Tis of Thee." There sat that magnificent
instrument, which could have filled the house with glorious music,
but all you ever heard from it was one little song, rather hesitatingly

rendered. It's a parable of Easter you know. That event which today we celebrate is capable of filling all our lives all of the time with glorious music. But instead, all the use we make of it is to play one little tune once in a while.

To illustrate what I mean, suppose we have a look at the episode in which these words were first spoken. Outside the circle of his disciples, our Lord had no closer friends than that family in Bethany. Lazarus, Martha, and Mary were almost like his own brothers and sisters, and their home in Bethany more congenial than his own home in Nazareth. And then word came one day that Lazarus was gravely ill. By the time that Jesus and his disciples got to Bethany (and his delay seems to have been quite deliberate), the funeral had been held. Martha, who met him by the grave, was a little disturbed that Jesus had not come sooner. Things might have been different if he had got there before Lazarus died. And when Jesus said, "But your brother will rise again," Martha answered in the terms of conventional piety, "I know that; he will rise again at the last day." It was then and in reply to that that our Lord spoke these words (and I paraphrase), "No, Martha; it's not a question of some future date; it's a question of the present, a matter of the now. I am the resurrection and the life. And if a person believes in me, that person lives and never dies. Do you believe that?"

It seems to me that this Easter morning most of us are no further along than Martha was. For how many people is Easter a kind of Memorial Day, when the dead are to be remembered, their graves decorated, and the ancient hope renewed that someday in a beautiful isle of somewhere we shall meet again. Ask not the average person in the street, but the average person in the pew who presumably has heard the Easter gospel time and again, ask what Easter is all about, and this is what you will be told. It commemorates the resurrection of Jesus Christ. And more likely than not, that person will go on to say that it gives promise of immortality, of life after death for us. Easter looks backward to that morning when the stone was rolled away, and it looks forward to that distant day when the dead shall rise, but it has very little to say to the immediate moment in which we live.

Like Martha, we only know that someday the dead shall live again. Like the child with the piano, we only know one tune. We are totally unprepared for our Lord's startling use of the present tense, *I am the resurrection and the life. Believest thou this?*

To begin to believe it, we have to understand that from the Christian point of view, life is far more than our physical existence and death much greater than its termination. From our point of view the distinction between life and death is an easy one to make. From the Christian point of view, it is a very subtle one. From the Christian point of view, scores of people whom we should call living are completely dead, while those whom we think of as dead are alive forevermore. The first thing that Easter has to tell us is that the difference between life and death is something more than a tombstone. Because of Easter, in the deepest and truest sense of the word, the difference between life and death is Jesus Christ. *I am the resurrection and the life: he that believeth in me, though he were dead, yet shall he live: And whosoever liveth and believeth in me shall never die. Believest thou this?*

Our Lord Jesus Christ came to redeem a world that had died inside. What disturbed him was not that men and women died and went to their graves, but that they died and went right on living. What disturbed him was that people became so insensitive to goodness, so dulled to love and mercy, so unconscious of faith and hope, so unaware of God that they could only be described as dead. Physically, they still existed; they ate, they slept, they laughed and cried, they played and worked. But in everything that makes them human and not just a higher animal, in everything that marks them as children of God and not creatures of the dust, they were dead. And what Jesus came to do was to bring the world back to life, to make men and women alive once again to all that matters, to all that lifts them above the contradictions and confusion, to all that gives them the spirit and the heart and the outlook of God's children. *I am the resurrection and the life.*

And it was on Easter that he finally did it. Will you forget for the moment that on Easter Jesus came back from the dead. That is the least important part of it, or rather, it is a part of the story that has meaning only as the result of these other more significant parts of the story. The Good Friday now past had simply confirmed what most people had suspected, what most people had been living, all along. Righteousness and mercy, love and hope, faith and trust— they are dead. They may feebly flicker for a time; but put them in any kind of show-down with the real powers in this world, selfishness and success, pride and passion, and you see what happens. They don't have a chance; they have neither the weapons nor even the will to fight. It is all very well to bid people to live by righteousness and mercy, to live by faith and hope. But here is proof, if indeed proof were necessary, that in this real world of struggle and striving, to bid them to live that way is to invite them to commit suicide. The limits of life, after all, are what you can touch and taste, what you can handle and feel, what you can have and hold in your possession. And for those things justice and mercy, love and hope are worse than useless.

That's how they had figured it then, those wise ones. And that's how they still have it figured today. They may still decorate life with a little religion. Crosses make pretty necklaces and churches add something to our city streets. But in the actual rough and tumble of living, of getting and spending, and above all of keeping, we know better. You have to push and shove; you have to defend yourself; you have to be hard and ruthless; you have to make people respect you. No time for tenderness or conscience, no time for the bleeding heart or the sensitive spirit. Life is short and the stakes are high. And so we drag out our lives, torn with strife, battered with struggle, worn with weary effort to hang on to things that keep slipping through our grasp.

And then it's Easter. Can you begin to feel how revolutionary this day is, how it literally reverses all of our most cherished convictions? The living Christ who meets us this morning in Joseph's garden shatters all of our precious ideas about life and turns them around. The very things that we think are strong his living presence declares to be weak. The very things that we assume are alive his glorious resurrection says are dead. The selfishness and greed, the lust and lying that waved their banners so triumphantly on Calvary, that screamed what they thought was the last word—now you see them for what they really are, defeated, finished, dead. And the goodness and mercy, the righteousness, and hope, the peace and love which we had so contemptuously dismissed as useless—now you see them for what they really are, unconquerable, invincible, alive. The deepest miracle of Easter morning is not the resurrection of life from death. The deepest miracle on Easter morning is the resurrection of goodness from evil, of faith from doubt, of hope from despair, of love from hate.

No, not even that is quite the truth. The deepest miracle on Easter morning is a countless host of men and women who, in the power of this event that shatters our ideas and reverses the trend of our history, die—die to the low aims, the selfish ambitions, the proud passions that have blocked their lives—and come alive, alive to the goodness and mercy, the love and righteousness, the faith and hope, the peace and power that are the birthright of the children of God. In the new world of Easter, in the new light of Easter, at last we see things as they really are; we come out of the shadows and delusions in which we have been groping our way, out into the brilliance of the world as God meant it and made it to be. And look—that hellish combination of selfishness, pride, and hate which have seduced us, ruined us, destroyed us—they are dead. And that glorious cluster of radiant qualities, hope and mercy and love and faith, which we have scorned and passed by—they are alive. *I am the resurrection and the life.*

And because that is true—and only because that is true—do we dare go on to make the next breath-taking assertion. *Whosoever liveth and believeth in me shall never die.* You see, we worry about life after death far too much, and about life here and now far too little. If life after death were but the prolongation into eternity of this poor beaten and bedraggled existence that we spell out here, who would want it? There is no Easter for that. But once our lives here and now have become permeated with these enduring and victorious qualities, once they have begun to breathe the atmosphere of faith and hope, the clean, pure air of trust and love, they cannot die. No more than the nails and the cross could destroy them at Calvary can the dissolution of this mortal body destroy them now. *Whosoever liveth and believeth in me shall never die.* Yes, the body, being composed of the elements of this earth, can and will die. But God, having created this one, can easily create a new one; 'tis a very small thing for him. But the life, the personality, the spirit, if you like, that radiates with the victorious qualities of Easter, that believes in Jesus, shall never die. How can it? His life is love and goodness and joy and peace; and these are things that shall outlast the world, because these are the things of God who is without beginning and without end.

But now; all during this Lent we have been considering some of the questions that Jesus asked. And we dare not forget that this tremendous Easter assertion also ends with a question, an eternal question. *Believest thou this?* And I must be very careful to let you know the full implications of that question. Our Lord is not asking us whether we think that all this is so, which is an easy thing to do, especially on a beautiful Easter morning when the blue sky seems just a little nearer earth than at any other time of the year. Nor is he asking us whether we find ourselves sympathetic to the idea, which doubtless we do. No, *believest thou this?* Are you willing to vote for it with your life? Are you ready to sink your foundations here? Are you able to trust the Easter gospel and stand by it in the dead and cold of winter?

For, mark you, if you do, there will be much in life to tempt you from it, much to argue and argue powerfully that it is not so, that it is all a lie. Not only will there be the seductive call of cheap success and easy gain, the siren voice of lazy comfort and least resistance; not only will there be the mocking taunts and the knowing glances of the wise world as it passes you on its mad rush to get ahead; there will be the bitter lashes of suffering, the stabbing wounds of pain, the numbing ache of death. Then—not in church on an Easter morning—but then, *believest thou this?* Then it is that fixing our eyes upon him whom sin could not break, hell could not capture, and death could not hold, we can triumphantly reply, even from our Calvaries, even from our graves, "I believe, I know that my redeemer liveth."   .

Matthew Arnold tells in one of his sonnets how one day in the slums of London, he met a college friend who was now a preacher in that god-forsaken part of the city. He was struck by the fact that his was the only happy face he had seen that whole day, and when he asked how it was that in this grim setting he could still look so radiant, his friend replied that it was because he was nourished by Christ, the living bread. And even though Matthew Arnold could not accept the Christian creed, this was his comment:

> "O human soul, so long as thou canst so
> Set up a mark of everlasting light
> Above the howling senses ebb and flow,
> To cheer thee and to right thee if thou roam,
> Not with lost toil thou laborest through the night
> Thou makst the heaven thou hopst indeed thy home."

That's Easter! It sets up a mark of everlasting light and in that light we discover the greatest miracle of all—the heaven for which we hope is already here our home!

I am the resurrection and the life: he that believeth in me, though he were dead, yet shall he live: And whosoever liveth and believeth in me shall never die. Believest thou this?

Preached at the North Reformed Church, Newark, New Jersey, March 29, 1959.

29

Easter Sunday V

*If ye then be risen with Christ, seek those things which
are above.*
Colossians 3:1

If ye then be risen with Christ—but what a very big if! For the vast
majority of the Christian world, I fancy, will have turned out in force
this Easter Day to celebrate not the present but the future. What is
Easter all about? Were I to ask you to answer that question, most
of you, I have no doubt, would unhesitatingly reply, the hope of
immortality. Because Jesus Christ lives, we too shall live. And we
have gathered here this morning because we want that hope
reconfirmed and renewed, because through the mists of time and
the shadows of space we want once again to catch a glimpse of that
light that shines brightly on another shore. We want to be told again
about that better country, that true native land of the human heart,
that beautiful isle of somewhere in which someday we shall all be
reunited. This is Easter as we understand it, Easter as we keep it; I
suspect it is also Easter as we want it—one day in the year that
speaks to us of another world without any reference, without any
relevance to this one in which we must spend the other 364. Easter,
the feast of immortality!

Now I certainly have no desire this Easter Day to deny that much of this which concerns us this morning is in the gospel, is part of the faith. Nor would I in any way seek to rob those whom sorrow has taken of the comfort of this hope. But I do have to say that when the New Testament comes to talk about Easter and its meaning, it never talks in the future; it always talks in the present. The gospel says much less about the Easter hope than it does about the Easter reality. Look, for example, at St. Paul's exhortation to his friends in Colossae. *If ye then be risen with Christ.* He is not talking to a cemetery, but to a city. Nor is he talking about what shall happen someday. He does not say, "When that great and final day comes in which you shall be risen with Christ." *If ye then be risen with Christ,* now, today, then certain things must follow.

But before we have a look at those things, we had best spend some time with the "if," the big If. For if St. Paul is right, we have not come here this Easter to be reminded of what is going to happen, but to celebrate what has happened, and happened to us. We are risen with Christ. Yes, you and I, living in the mid-twentieth century with all of its fears and contradictions, all of its anxieties and tensions, all of its problems and pains, you and I, living right here in this world, are living in it as completely new and transformed people. This is the Easter miracle—not what will happen there, but what has happened, what can happen now. And if you and I do not sense that miracle, if our hearts have not been grasped by it, then no amount of day-dreaming about the beautiful isle of somewhere will ever make Easter real. For Easter is not for the next world; it is for this one, *if ye then be risen with Christ.*

Here then is our first responsibility on Easter Day—to persuade ourselves, or persuade ourselves again as the case may be, of the new possibilities for existence, the new dimensions of living which Easter has opened for us. We need to see once again and see more clearly that Easter is the root out of which a whole new way of life can grow. When our blessed Lord revealed himself alive to his disciples that first Easter Day, nothing was said about immortality

or the life of the world to come. You will search the record in vain
for so much as a hint that that was the issue. But everything was said
about the new possibilities which now they had for life in this world.
Because he had risen from the dead and was alive, the fears and the
anxieties, the limitations and uncertainties which had crippled and
spoiled their lives in this world were broken. Those gates of iron
which had been so tightly closed against every possibility of a life of
faith, hope, and trust were now shattered. Because of Easter, we can
trust and not be frightened; because of Easter, we can hope and not
be ashamed; because of Easter, we can love and not be anxious ...
if ye then be risen with Christ.

But we have tarried long enough with the If. The time has come
to look at the results, the tremendous results of the event that we
celebrate today. The time has come to examine the blossoms that
grow on this new root, the root of Easter. And they can all be
summarized this way: Because of Easter, in any earthly situation the
only real possibility is now the heavenly one. Because of Easter, in
any human choice the only real decision is the heavenly one.
Because of Easter, in any earthly uncertainty, the only real certainty
is the heavenly one. What a tremendous dynamic for life. Because
of Easter, you can be sure wherever you look in life that the only
lasting, certain, unshakable reality is the heavenly reality. You can
put your life down on it and never be afraid of the consequences.
Easter is the root that blossoms in the sky. *If ye then be risen with Christ,
seek those things which are above .... Set your affection on things above, not on
things on the earth.*

Well, there is the Easter assertion in all of its splendor. Should we
spend a few moments looking at it a little more closely, examining
it perhaps in some of its particulars? We have come here this Easter
Day, many of us, feeling very discouraged about the world in which
we live. It is a strange world, vastly unlike the simple world of black
and white, of right and wrong, in which we were brought up. Its
tragedy and its terror have begun to haunt us. That simple faith
which we learned as children seems so impractical, so unrealistic in

a world of power blocs, of massive economic dishonesty, of savage competition, of ruthless destruction. When you must listen every day to its noise and clamor, when you are caught in its toils and dragged with it, how pathetically feeble, how curiously unreal the little Christian maxims sound! Goodness, forgiveness, kindness—in a world like this? It sounds pretty silly, doesn't it? No wonder that thousands of people have given the whole Christian thing up as foolishness, that thousands more, while they keep it, keep it as a little shrine carefully isolated from the business of daily life. Haven't you ever felt like doing the same thing yourself?

But now it's Easter, and Easter, remember, is the guarantee that in any situation the only real possibility is the heavenly possibility. Yes, even in the world in which we live, the mad, confused, sick world of the twentieth century. My conscience, how we need Easter! We need it to put some perspective in our picture of life, need it to re-establish our lost loyalties to the only things that matter. For we come here this Easter Day as those who have compromised, betrayed, denied. And we need to know that that way lies destruction only; this way only lies life. Decorate it with all the twentieth-century language that you will, what we are doing is the same foolish thing that people have always done. And when we shall have involved our world in the doom that that way of life always brings, the simple clean goodness of Easter will still be real. Heavenly possibilities are the only real possibilities. Don't quit them for any lesser good! *If ye then be risen with Christ, seek those things which are above.*

We have come here this Easter Day, many of us, discouraged about ourselves. The fears, the anxieties, the problems, the burdens of day-to-day existence are almost too much for us. We welcome this little oasis in life's desert, the carols, the flowers, the alleluias. It is like the echo of a song we used to be able to sing; but now our hearts are muted. We almost dread to go back to tomorrow because we know what we are going to find there; we know, because we left it there yesterday. Domine, you might as well know. These words on which you ring the changes, hope, faith, trust, love, victory—

what do they mean in our situation? We have tried them. But how can a broken heart love? How can a shattered spirit hope? How can a frightened soul trust? The terror of life is too much for the thin and fragile optimism of your gospel. What can you say to the brokenness, the loneliness, the anxiety of our lives?

I can say only this. Today is Easter. And Easter, remember, is the guarantee that in any situation the only real possibility is the heavenly possibility. And that means most basically, my friend, that we need to believe that even in the lostness of our lives there are heavenly possibilities. Who would have believed at three o'clock on Good Friday that there was any heavenly possibility whatever in that awful scene of murder and death. Not even the world's most incurable optimist could have seen it! But one man persisted in that faith, even when every bit of evidence was against him, even when he was drawing his last breath. And because Jesus Christ never lost his faith in the heavenly possibility, three days later there was an Easter.

Now here is that same Easter to say to us in our desperation not only that even in our lostness and brokenness, even in our Calvaries, there are heavenly possibilities, but that these are the only real possibilities. Find them and cling to them we must. Whatever it may be that God is trying to say to you through your cross, you can be sure that he is trying to say something. Listen for it, because it is the only thing worth hearing. Even in what may seem to you thick darkness, there are treasures. The blossom in the sky is possible even from what may seem to you a very dry root. Out of these sorrows, you can make songs. From this trouble and discouragement, you can shape new dimensions of personality. O, if there had been no Easter, I could only say, "Face it bravely and take your chances." But because of Easter I can say, "Even the heaviest cross is a gate to new possibilities." *If ye then be risen with Christ, seek those things which are above.*

We have come here this Easter Day, all of us, though some more recently, more keenly than others, feeling the sharpness of death.

And philosophize about it as we will, when it brushes close to you, it is an ugly thing. In that awful stillness that follows the final breaking of the cord, there are so many unanswered questions, so many unresolved doubts, so many unfathomed mysteries. "Death, where is thy triumph? Grave, where is thy victory?" We know the answer only too well. The triumph and the victory are seared deeply in the sorrow of our hearts, the loneliness of our lives. Much as we knew that it had to come, it never came at the right moment, did it? The numbness has never quite left our souls; the questions will never entirely leave our minds.

But today is Easter. And Easter, remember, is the guarantee that in any situation the only real possibility is the heavenly possibility. Is that true here? Yes, it is true here. For the heavenly possibility, the only possibility in the finality of this situation, is God. The longer we dwell with ourselves, speculating as to our chances for surviving this shock that sunders body from spirit, the more hopelessly confused we become. But the more we can fix our attention on God who made us, asking about the possibility that in his love he will remake us, the more light we see, even in the darkness. Has God not been remaking us all along the way, making the crooked straight and the rough plain in our lives, leveling the mountains of our pride, raising the deep valleys of our despair and doubt? Do not ask about the possibility of new life there unless you are certain about the possibility of new life here. But if in the deep experiences of your own heart you have felt the molding hand of God whose touch transforms, then Easter must make sense to you, make sense as the continuation of what he has been doing all along, the completing of what has been his great design with you from the very beginning.

And once you have seen that possibility, how it changes the whole face of death. But is there really any other possibility? Either nothing, blank, faceless nothing, or this, that God who has used every cross to mold me is both able and willing to make even death a transforming experience of life. Yes, even by an open grave in the cemetery, ours is the root that blossoms in the sky. Even there, the heavenly possibility is still the only reality. *If ye then be risen with Christ, seek those things which are above.*

What should Easter mean to us? It should mean that Monday morning, the dry dead pieces of existence come alive with freshness and grace and beauty. It should mean that the drabness and dullness of our existence are radiant with possibilities of glory. It should mean that the heaviness of sorrow and heartache shine with the glow of victory. It should mean courage, hope, life. Christ is risen! Yes, thank God. But I have risen too; even though my life is on earth, my heart is in the sky!

> Then alleluia all my gashes cry:
> My woe springs up and flourishes from the tomb
> In her lord's likeness, terrible and fair:
> Knowing her root, her blossom in the sky
> She rears: now flocking to her branches come
> The paradisal birds of upper air,
> Which alleluia cry and cry again
> And death from out the grave replies amen.[1]

If ye then be risen with Christ, seek those things which are above.

Preached at the North Reformed Church, Newark, New Jersey, April 2, 1961.

1   Ruth Pitter, *A Solemn Meditation*, 1897.

30

Easter Sunday VI

I am he that liveth, and was dead; and, behold, I am alive forever more and have the keys of hell and of death.
Revelation 1:18

Some sixty years had passed since the first Easter Day. Of the eleven men who had been sitting panic-stricken in an upper room in Jerusalem when their master had come back to them from the dead, there was but one left now, and he was a lonely old man in dreary exile on the rocky and desolate island of Patmos. Separated from all his Christian brothers and sisters, sent out there to die by the harsh imperial authority, he found very little hope or encouragement when he thought of the future. Those glorious days when they had walked and talked with the master in Galilee, they were now in the distant past. That wonderful morning when the incredible news had come to their doubting ears that their Christ had conquered death and was alive, that was now just a dimming memory. The fresh enthusiasm in which they had set out with the good news of his triumph on their lips, that was only a slowly fading glow. To John as he sat alone in his island prison the future seemed very dark indeed. Arrayed against the little handful of Christian people was the great strength of the Roman Empire, crushing the life out of them. And even in the little scattered company there were some who were secretly disloyal, some who were indifferent and apathetic, some who had no courage to endure. It seemed as though everything for which John had given up his whole life was going to be lost. What chance did so few have against the determined opposition of a whole empire? And so on the very anniversary of the day on which his Lord had risen from the dead, John sat looking out on a world in which everything was going wrong.

And while he was sitting there filled with such gloomy forebodings, suddenly he became aware of a mighty presence with him. It shone with a power and blazed with a glory so brilliant that he could not bear to look at it, but fell down on his face blinded by its radiance. And then to John, sick at heart with worry and fear, there came a voice that spoke with the thunderous sound of a great waterfall. "Fear not, I am he that liveth, and was dead; and behold I have the keys of hell and death!" And there with his lonely and fearful disciple was no man of sorrows, no fading memory, no lost and far-off glory, but the living Christ of triumph and of power.

What an Easter message there is here for you and me! For in more ways than one you and I are like John on his lonely island of Patmos. O to be sure, we know the Easter story, we are aware that Christ rose from the dead. But it seems such a long way back to all that! So many centuries have come in between us and him, so many things have happened in the world since light's glittering morn bedecked that sky that the glory and the wonder and the power have dimmed and faded. Easter is there all right, but it is way in the background of our living. And when, once a year, it is pushed for a time into the foreground of our thinking, it quickly slips back again and for another year is almost lost to us. We have such difficulty in conjuring up enough imagination to travel back there to Joseph's lovely garden to recapture what must have been the wonder of that first Easter Day let alone holding onto it.

At the same time, when we turn our minds toward the future, how troubled and concerned we become! It is not easy to see very many rays of light peeping through the dark clouds that hang over our pathways. It is not even easy to convince ourselves that we have a future. How pathetically few people seem to be genuinely concerned about the things that make for peace and righteousness! In contrast with the countless hordes of those who live only to eat, drink, and make merry, how weak and enfeebled is the company of those who have put first the kingdom of God and his righteousness. What is to become of our world? Yes, and what is to become of us? Here we are, helpless in the face of economic insecurity, of personal frustration, caught in a time of conflict and tension from which there seems to be no escape. Gone forever are the days when people could quietly tend to their own business and leave the world outside to those who cared about it. Now that same world exerts its pressure upon every moment of our life, wearying us with its strife and cruelty, yet never granting us a moment's rest from its uneasiness and its uncertainty.

Isn't that where we are? The Easter story itself is too distant, too unreal for us to have much confidence in it. And the future is too dark and too uncertain for us to have much confidence in it either! So if we are going to have any confidence, any nerve for living at all, we have to find something in the present, in the now, in which we can put our trust, on which we can rely. That's what we want most of all, isn't it? Floundering about in life's uncertainty and confusion, we want something which we can grasp and know that it will hold, something solid on which we can let our lives down and know that they will be supported, something that will restore confidence and assurance to our living, something that will give us a guide into the future, something that will give us a key with which to unlock the doors before us that now seem closed. What right now can we find as a confident and sure clue to life? In what can we put our trust and be certain that we shall not be afraid or ashamed?

Dr. R. W. Dale, the great Birmingham preacher, tells somewhere of an experience which came to him as he was preparing for an Easter sermon.

> "Christ is alive," I said to myself; alive—and then I paused;— alive, and then I paused again.—alive! Can that really be true? living as really as I myself am? I got up and walked about repeating, Christ is living, Christ is living. At first it seemed strange and hardly true, but at last it came upon me as a burst of sudden glory.

There is the key to the future. There is the confidence and strength, the nerve for life that we want and need. Not in armies and air forces, not in machines and industrial might, not in economic blueprints and government planning, but there in that tremendous assertion and realization, Christ is living! When we have discovered that Easter tells not just of someone who rose from the dead in an ancient garden, not merely of a far away miracle in a distant place, but that it tells of a living presence in life's now, then we have the keys of the kingdom. *I am he that liveth, and was dead, and behold, I am alive forever more and have the keys of hell and death.*

My friends, in the same power and in the same dazzling glory, this Easter Day Christ stands over against our lives even as he stood next to John. We *are* troubled and anxious about the future. The world is dark and uncertain and we can't find our way through it. We see the things that we have held dear going down to apparent defeat. We see the standards that we have tried to hold up mocked and sneered at. We see the way of life in which we believe questioned and denied. We see the values which we think are real ignored and neglected. We see the principles for which we have fought attacked and beaten. And in our heart of hearts we cry out, What is the use, My God, what is the use? Does anybody care for these things any more?

Don't be afraid. I was dead. The standards which I brought, the values which I taught, the way of life which I lived, they were all taken out to Calvary and nailed up there in blood. And the world washed its hands and said, now, we are through with those things! But God wasn't through. I am alive again and I am here to stay! And your values, and your standards, and your way of life, give them to me and let me keep them, for the future is mine. I have the keys of hell and of death.

Or he comes to us and he finds us weeping like Magdalene at the tomb. Life no longer has any sense or meaning. It has robbed us of the few guideposts that we had left so that we no longer know where we are going or care. Once we started out with high objectives and great ideals. Our lives were led on by a glorious vision of what they might be. But now they have become so tarnished and dirty that we no longer can see them. And we no longer have anything to live for, no more great hopes, no more great promises, no more great expectations. We simply go on living from day to day, picking up the loose strands of life and trying to piece them into something as we go. Ours is the ultimate tragedy of lost goals and vanished ideals and we think it is too late to do anything about it.

Don't be afraid. I was dead. The hopes and the dreams and the promises that lifted the weary heart in my life, they were all blasted and destroyed as the nails were driven through my hands and the spear was thrust into my side. And the world said, now we will live without dreams, without hopes, without visions. But I am alive again! The future is mine. Entrust your dreams, your hopes, your ideals to me. I can keep them safe, for I have the keys of hell and death.

Or he comes to us in an hour of sorrow. People whom we held dear have slipped away from us into that unknown country from which there is no returning. As we try to follow them out into the great beyond, our hearts grow heavy and perhaps our spirits grow bitter. Where have they gone? Is there anything after this, or are all our ideas of another life only illusions with which we deceive ourselves? If only they could come back to us, only for a moment,

to let us know that they are still living and happy. But when we turn
to look for such an answer, there comes only a fearful silence that
tells us nothing.

Don't be afraid. I was dead. I too went down and crossed that
dark river. My broken and bruised body was laid in a grave and the
stone was rolled across it. And everyone said, Well now, he's
finished. We'll hear no more from him. We can forget him. That's
the end of him. But I am alive again and the future is mine. You
can put those that you have loved and lost safely in my keeping. I
live and so shall they. I have the keys of hell and death.

Long ago, we know not when nor where, there was written a very
curious book entitled, *The Gospel According to Nicodemus.* In very
picturesque language it describes how Jesus Christ attacked and
conquered hell. There heavily fortified and closely guarded was the
citadel wherein dwelt all of the ugly powers and evil forces that prey
upon human life to hurt and destroy it. Marching down toward that
fortress came the Christ carrying his cross. There at the doorway
two devils held their flaming swords to bar his entrance, but when
he held up his cross their swords shattered and dropped from their
hands.

Inside Satan was laughing with his lieutenants over the way in
which he had been able to kill Jesus, when all of a sudden outside
the gate there came a thundering voice, "Lift up your heads, O ye
gates, and be ye lifted up, ye everlasting doors, that the king of glory
may come in." In utter consternation the powers of evil within
cried out, "But who is the king of glory?" And there came back at
once the answer, as with the voice of ten thousand trumpets, "The
Lord of hosts, the Lord strong and mighty in battle." And then
straightway at his word, the gates of brass were broken in pieces and
the bars of iron were ground to powder and for all time spirits were
set free!

What a parable of Easter's real meaning. Into our lives, bound by
fear, chained by evil, enslaved to doubt and sin and death comes the
shout of the conquering king. Lift up your heads and let the king

of glory, the Lord strong and mighty, come in. He holds the keys of the kingdom and the future, our future, belongs to him. *I am he that was dead, and behold I am alive forevermore and have the keys of hell and death.*

Preached at Christ Community Church, Denver, Colorado, April 24, 1977; Garfield Park Reformed Church, Grand Rapids, Michigan, April 18, 1982; and Second Reformed Church, Coxsackie, New York, April 7, 1985.

Part V

Ascension Day

31

Ascension Day I

Go to my brethren, and say unto them, I ascend unto my
Father, and your Father; and to my God and your God.
 John 20:17

I have often wondered why it should be that the observance of
Ascension Day has come upon such evil days in our Protestant
communities. With the exception of a handful of churches, Ascension
Day will pass unnoticed by most of the Protestant people in this or
in any other community. And while it is true that among our Roman
Catholic friends the day is still kept, I really wonder how serious an
observance it is. Just this morning, for example, I was listening on
the radio to one of those couples whose breakfast table conversation
is broadcast. They are announced and declared Roman Catholics
who make a great show of loyalty to their church. And yet this
morning, when their little daughter appeared and said that she was
not going to school because it was a feast day, neither her father nor
her mother knew what feast day it was. I suppose it is the fact that
Ascension Day always comes on a Thursday, together with the fact
that it has no family customs or folk traditions like Christmas or
Easter, that is largely responsible for its neglect. Nor would I simply
lament the neglect of the day, as though there were some peculiar

virtue in observing days for their own sake. What troubles me is
rather that in forgetting Ascension Day we too often forget the
truth which the day is meant to enshrine and so lose one of the stable
elements in our faith.

If Ascension Day were nothing but the remembrance of the fact
that on a particular Thursday, forty days after Easter, our Lord, by
means which we can neither understand or explain, ascended into
heaven, though it might have a certain historical interest, I do not
suppose it would be worth a great deal of our attention. One might
argue that after all, since his resurrection from the dead, it was
necessary to get Jesus Christ off the scene somehow and the
ascension provided as good a means as any. For obviously he is not
here now in any visible form. I dare say that that is all that the
Ascension does mean to a great many people—nothing but the way
in which our Lord left us. But I am also certain that to see in this day
no deeper meaning than that is not only to lose the real significance
of the day, but to lose some of the most important Christian
assertions about life as well.

It may seem like a small thing, but I think I can get at what I mean
by calling to your attention the fact that in announcing his Ascension
to Mary Magdalene in the words of the text, our Lord did not say,
"I ascend unto my Father and to my God." He was about to do that
certainly, and if his ascension had been no more than his removal
from the scene of his earthly labors, those words would have been
quite sufficient. But that is not what he said. "I ascend unto my
Father and your Father and to my God and your God," were his
words. And the inclusion of us in his statement makes all the
difference in the world.

You see, the real significance of Ascension Day is not simply or
even principally in its account of what happened to Jesus Christ, but
rather in its assertion about the nature and destiny of us all. The
Ascension is a dramatic proclamation of the faith and the fact that
journey's end for humankind is God, that the purpose and the
destiny for which we are being shaped is in God *my Father and your*

Father, my God and your God. Our Lord's Ascension to his Father is nothing but the striking symbol of the final destiny of your life and mine. It was for God that you were made and it is to God that finally you shall go.

I hardly think that this is a point that needs stressing in times like these. In the evening psalm we read those striking words, "What is man that thou art mindful of him or the son of man that thou visitest him? For thou hast made him a little lower than the angels, and hast crowned him with glory and honor." Magnificent words those, stunning assertions about the meaning of human nature. And yet you know how hard they are to believe in a world like ours in which we behave like the beasts of the field and the brutes of the forest! Our inhumanity to others, our fury, our cruelty, our dark passion and low crime, our lurid ambitions—they do not add up to very impressive evidence for our being a little lower than the angels, do they? Go to the library, if your stomach can stand it, and get out one of the books of pictures that were taken in Dachau or Buchenwald by the Allies soon after their arrival in those dens, look at the half-starved, bruised, and beaten creatures who were all made that way by the deliberate cruelty of other human beings. What will you say of human nature when you have shut that volume?

Doubtless it was the case that a few short years ago we had almost limitless faith in the divine possibilities of human nature. But today, unless I am very much mistaken, our mood and temper are rather distrust and cynicism. Our modern novelists seem intent upon reminding us of the filth and the crudity of human life. Our modern psychologists never weary of calling to our attention our kinship with the lower animals. And surely most of our modern activities do little but reinforce their point of view. Conscious as we are of the smut and the dirt of life, the fickleness and instability of human character, the dark passions and unpredictable lusts that lurk beneath the surface of human personality, we have very little patience with those who put their faith in human beings. Our destiny, so far as we can tell, if we manage to avoid self-destruction, is not in the stars, but in the dust.

Now I do not want to imply that the Christian faith takes any falsely optimistic view about human nature or that it tries to pretend that we are better than we are. The startling thing about the Christian faith is that though it is perfectly honest about us as we are, sees all the dirt and smut, knows all the weakness and failure, nevertheless it still dares to assert that our final destiny is in God. Faced with the shabbiest life and the tawdriest personality, the gospel still maintains that that life and that personality have meaning, purpose, and significance waiting for them in God. That's the meaning of the Ascension. It is God's declared will, his revealed purpose to take our dull and plodding lives and by the persuasive power of love lift them to his level, his quality of life. I admit that whoever looks at human nature as it is can find very little cause for hope and very much cause for despair. Indeed, when we look honestly at ourselves we will find very little hope and much despair. But the message of Ascension Day is that whoever looks at human beings as they are is only looking at half the truth.

This is what is so discouraging about our novelists, our historians, and our psychologists. They pile up all kinds of damning evidence as to our bestiality. Of course, in a world like this, they do not have much trouble in doing it. A novelist like James Jones will write sordid page after sordid page of life in the army and say, "This is realism." Or a historian will describe all of the horrors, the atrocities, the indecencies of national or political life and say, "This is realism." Or a psychologist will collect data on all of the irrational and inhuman thoughts that we think and say, "This is realism." But it is not realism—that's the Christian answer—it is not realism. It is a highly distorted and one-sided view of human nature, because it leaves out the great fact of God. Let the novelist write the story of an Albert Schweitzer or a Father Damien, men whose passions were over-mastered by the great passion of God to help and to heal. Are they less real than the shabby figures of a modern novel? Or let the historian chronicle the selfless devotion of the Salvation Army, for surely that army is no less real than the German army or the Russian. Let the psychologist analyze the motives of those who master their lower selves, resist their temptations, and march out into life to do something creative and constructive. Are their personalities possessed of less reality than the homicidal maniac or the sex pervert?

You see, we are concerned here with far more than the mere observance of a day. We are concerned with the most basic question which we can ask. Who are we? It has always been a pressing question, but never more so than at this moment when the tendency is to discredit humanity and to write it off as a fruitless and freakish variant in the evolutionary process. I have heard responsible people state that a bird is by any standards a higher physical specimen than a human. I have read articles by intelligent people arguing that the social life of an ant or a bee was on a much higher basis than that of a human being. And against all this kind of thing, the only effective protest that I know is the witness of the Christian gospel with its proclamation that despite our rebellion and sin, we will be lifted by the love of God to new levels of living and new qualities of character.

It is a mystery, of course, which I should not profess to be able to explain. But the clear meaning of the Ascension is that in some way or other humanity is now in the heart of God. When we say in the Apostles' Creed, "He sitteth at the right hand of God," of course, we all know that God has no right hand and he is not literally sitting anywhere. The right hand always stands for the place of power and honor. To say that Jesus Christ sits at the right hand of God is simply to say that in him humanity is nearest to the mind and heart of God. "My Father and your Father, my God and your God" is no remote and awful impersonal power who knows nothing and cares less about what happens in this earthly experiment, but one who has identified completely with this earthly experiment and will not rest until it has been worked out to his will and purpose.

If it is true that Christians believe in God, it is also true that Christians believe in humanity, and believe as no other people can. Christians believe in people, not for what we are or do, but for what we will be made by the grace and the power of God. Journey's end for human life is neither the cemetery nor self-destruction, but God. Just as he lifted Christ to himself, so it is his will to lift you and me above the confusion and failures of our lives, out of the mistakes and failures of our hearts, up to God's way of life. So long as there is a God on the throne of the universe, human destiny lies not with the scum but with the sky. That is the message and meaning of Ascension Day.

It is not without significance, I think, that our Lord prefaced this statement about his Ascension with a command. *Go to my brethren and say unto them.* Of course, in its narrower sense it was simply a directive to Magdalene to inform the twelve. But it has a wider sense which we dare not ignore. For if ever there were a message for which our hearts are hungering, it is the message of the Ascension. All around us people's faces are bowed in the dust, their hearts are heavy with despair, they have lost their courage and their nerve. They have lost their faith in any possibilities in life let alone in any divine ones. Not only have they lost their faith in God, they have lost their faith in themselves. What can help them, what can help us, but a renewal of faith in the lifting power of God in Jesus Christ? This is our responsibility—to proclaim the new possibilities that have been broken open for us in Jesus Christ, to proclaim them not simply by the sermons that we preach or the hymns that we sing, but by the lives that we live, lives that have themselves been lifted and made new. *Go to my brethren and say unto them, I ascend unto my Father, and your Father, and to my God, and your God.*

Preached at the North Reformed Church, Newark, New Jersey, May 14, 1953.

32

Ascension Day II

Seek those things which are above, where Christ sitteth on the right hand of God.
Colossians 3:1

I wonder whether you have ever been puzzled during the recitation of the Apostle's Creed to know exactly what is meant by the phrase, "the right hand of God." "He ascended into heaven and sitteth on the right hand of God the Father Almighty" we said a little while ago. Now what exactly did we mean? Or perhaps, more personally, what exactly did you mean? The language is, of course, pictorial. And the picture which it instantly suggests is that of a throne room with a dais at one end and on the dais a throne in which God the Father Almighty sits, looking very dignified. And over here on his right hand, seated on a chair at a somewhat lower level, is Jesus Christ. I do not mean to be crude, but I am very certain that that is the picture which comes to mind when most people say these words. Indeed, if these pictures be taken at their literal value, what other scene could come to their mind? Just as with the Ascension itself, which we celebrate today, the language of Scripture by its pictures suggests that Jesus went up and is now living and operating in another storey of the universe, so to speak, somewhere above the one in which you and I live.

Well, of course, we all realize, I hope, that these are pictures which were not intended to be and cannot be taken literally. God is a spirit; with neither right hand nor left hand. Indeed, He sits on no throne, because a Spirit does not occupy space. When our creed talks about sitting on the right hand of God, it is speaking in symbols, trying to express pictorially and graphically what is so high and so deep that it cannot really be expressed in any other way. The men who framed the creed knew that perfectly well. They knew the words of Jesus as well as you or I that "God is a Spirit and they who worship him must worship him in spirit and in truth." They knew that in the literal sense of the word, God has no right hand. If they chose this symbolic way of expressing truth which they could not express in any other way, it is your job and mine to try to grasp the meaning of the reality that lies behind the symbol, to lay hold upon the idea which has been clothed in these picturesque garments. What does it mean to say that Jesus sits on the right hand of God?

We can begin to understand its meaning, I think, if we remember that the world in which the men of the Bible lived was a world of absolute monarchs, kings and emperors who ruled in a pretty despotic fashion. But as you may know, kings themselves did very little of the actual business of governing. They may have made the decisions, but the execution of those decisions was up to someone else. They may have formed the plans, but the carrying out of the plans was generally entrusted to another; a prime minister, or a chancellor, or a grand wizard, or what have you. The title varied, but the office was the same. This official stood in the place of power between the king and the people. The job was to carry out the wishes of the throne; if you wished to approach the throne, it was a wise thing to make that approach through him.

Now what is more, in the etiquette of royal courts, this prime minister or chancellor always stood on the king's right. That was the station. I suppose that we still have something of the same idea when we say that so-and-so is our "right hand man." We mean, of course, not that this person is literally to be found on our right hand all the time, but that so far as we are concerned, he is in a relationship of responsibility to us. And if that be true in everyday speech, how much more true was it in court circles. To be on the right hand was to be in the place of power. Anyone in the day in which the New Testament was written would instantly have recognized in the phrase, "on the right hand," the equivalent of power and authority.

When the New Testament therefore seeks to describe the meaning and significance of Jesus Christ today, it naturally can find no more apt simile than to say, "He is on the right hand of God." Jesus Christ is not a pathetic and forgotten figure of long ago, not a mystic dreamer and visionary from the hills of Galilee, not a misunderstood martyr who was victimized by enemies. Jesus Christ is the expression of God's power and authority in this world today. That's the meaning of the Ascension; that's the meaning of the right hand of God. God's will for the world; the way in which that will shall be accomplished; God's goal for human living and the means by which that goal shall be achieved—you find and see them all in the living person of Jesus Christ. He is the way in which this universe is ruled.

Let me explore briefly what the Ascension means when thought of in those terms. If Jesus Christ is the power of God at this very moment, then only that which in our human situation is Christlike can be permanent. All the lesser goals which men and nations set themselves in the very nature of things will not and cannot last. I could, for example, say a great deal about the international scene in light of the Ascension. In the two thousand years of the history of our era, where is there one single state or nation alive to tell it which has consistently set itself un-Christlike goals? O, they had their temporary successes, their cheap glories, their brief swaggers across history's stage before they went to join the large company waiting them in the graveyard. Does it mean nothing that national immorality and selfishness and lust have spelled the doom of every nation that has followed them? Is it sheer accident that the Caesars and the Napoleons and the Hitlers have all been swept from history's stage in an agony of blood and tears? I think not. To me it is proof conclusive of the truth of the Ascension. King Jesus is on the throne. He sits at the right hand of God in the place of power and brings to naught all goals and purposes that are not in accordance with his will. Since he sits at the right hand of God, Jesus Christ is the only goal that history will permit. Remember that when you are tempted to think that God no longer rules in world affairs.

But it has its application also to our personal living, this Ascension gospel. For so often we yield to lesser goals and inferior purposes for ourselves. We pick the easy out, the convenient thing, the short-term happiness, the temporary advantage. Then we wonder why life seems empty, why so many people leave it feeling they have been cheated. If Jesus Christ is at the right hand of God in the place of power, then nothing less than his will can provide lasting strength and abiding satisfaction for any of our human lives. Whoever is contented with less than Jesus Christ's character, less than Jesus Christ's way, less than Jesus Christ's purposes, is self-doomed to failure in life. You will not find lasting peace in less than the purposes of Christ, real satisfaction in less than the goal of Christ. For he is at the right hand of God; he is the final power, the destiny, the goal of all things living.

And what has been said about ends can just as well be said about means. Not only is he the goal, but he is the only way to the goal. Not only will history tolerate no other purpose but him, it will tolerate no other way of reaching our purposes but his way. Love may seem a very long way around compared with the speed of hate; but only love will finally arrive. Truth may seem a terrible, difficult pathway compared with the ease of a lie; but only truth will finally take us to our destination. Kindness is an uphill pull compared with the easy slide of selfishness; but we shall reach our purposes by marching, not by sliding. Since Jesus Christ is at the right hand of God, the very stars in their courses are arrayed against those who try to use other methods, other means, other ways to reach their destination. Ever since he hung on it, the cross is the only way to glory.

I wonder how many battles must be fought, how many millions must go to their graves before the nations learn the truth? One after another they have tried to sail to power through a sea of blood, and they have never arrived, nor will they, can they. But I wonder even more how long it will take for us to learn it? Why do you suppose that Albert Schweitzer in his simple little hospital in French Equatorial Africa is a hundred times happier than most of us? Because, though he might not so state it, he has learned the truth of the Ascension gospel. He has learned that just as the only goal worth the effort is Christlikeness, so the only way to that goal is the way that Christ went, the way of love, forgiveness, kindness, gentleness, selflessness. There is no peace in a lie, no satisfaction in lust, no power in pretense, no victory in selfishness, and why? Because the power in this universe is set in a completely different direction. Those who use other methods to reach their goals will always find themselves stopped, not perhaps at once, but often abruptly and with a cruel shock. Those who walk his way will find that they have strength and patience and courage that they did not think they possessed. And it is so simply because his is the kingdom and the power and the glory forever. He is at the right hand of God, throwing his might against those who would pursue another course, but behind those who want to obey.

Now perhaps we can better understand the meaning of that word which the Apostle wrote to his friends in Colossae. *Seek those things which are above where Christ sitteth on the right hand of God.* In these human lives of ours, there are temptations and discouragements aplenty. We need more than a teacher from far-away Nazareth; we need more than a dead man hanging on a cross; we need what we have—the power of God summed up and concentrated in Jesus Christ. This is the Apostle's word. Don't go through life with your eyes on the ground and your mind on the earth. Look up! Don't be content with goals of your own devising, with the plans and the purposes sanctioned by the wisdom of this world. Don't spend your life on things like these. They are will-o-the-wisps which you will never catch. They never bring satisfaction, peace. *Seek the things above where God's power is.* Set before your mind and heart Christian goals and Christian purposes. They are much harder to reach, they are much further off. But they contain a peace which passes understanding and a joy which nothing can take from you. There is just one reason why you should be content with nothing less and his name is Jesus Christ.

Then, when in the thick of life's struggle and the heat and burden of its day, it seems so hard to love, to forgive, to be kind, and you feel like giving it all up and going the way of the world, *seek those things above where the power of God is.* Refresh and renew your weakness and discouragement in the life-giving strength that alone can take you where God wants you to go. His way is a hard way, but it is the only way. The means are difficult ones, but there are no others. The person whose heart is on the ground may easily be tempted to try a short-cut. But the person whose heart is above knows that only one road leads home, knows that though the travel may be rough, the power of God in Christ is always available for those who walk that way.

To say that Jesus Christ is at the right hand of God means this; there is no problem, no difficulty, no situation in this world in which, if we will but look and listen, Jesus does not have the final word. That's a faith by which you can live, in which you can die, and with which you can always triumph—because the triumph has already been won. Jesus can never be defeated. *Seek those things which are above where Christ sitteth on the right hand of God.*

Preached at the North Reformed Church, Newark, New Jersey, May 19, 1955.

33

Ascension Day III

It is not for you to know about dates or times which the Father has set within his own control. But you will receive power when the Holy Spirit comes upon you: and you will bear witness for me.
Acts 1:7-8

It was an unbelievable question the disciples had asked. After all the time they had spent with him, all the things they had heard him say, all the experiences they had had from Good Friday to Easter— after all that, here they are asking him if now was the time when Israel would once again become a free and sovereign nation! An unbelievable question! But if we think about ourselves a little bit, perhaps it is not so unbelievable after all. I know there are Christians today who are still busy trying to set dates for the end of the world and the return of Jesus Christ—and that in spite of his clear words that it is not for us to know about dates or times which the Father has set within his own control. I am not really thinking about them this Ascension Day night because I know that few if any of us fall within their category.

But I am thinking of the many ways in which you and I misunderstand Jesus Christ as what I might call a dead-end street. It's all over with; he's done it. All you and I have to do is to settle back and enjoy it. That's an exaggeration, an oversimplification

possibly, but it represents the attitude of so many Christian people.
Just look at what we have! We have a church, we have a faith, we
have reassurance and help in time of need. We have everything we
need and more to live happy, calm, and peaceful lives. To be sure,
we do not always make it, but we are the first to admit that that is
not his fault. It is ours for allowing the distractions of the world in
which we live to get in the way of our believing in him and taking
him seriously.

And in a way, you see, the Ascension which we are celebrating
tonight puts the capstone on the whole business. Now he is
enthroned in heaven, sitting on the right hand of God, with all
power in his hands. And that means that he is able to give us all that
we need whenever we ask for it. Let the world do with us as it will,
treat us as it will, we have Jesus Christ on our side, able to give us
more abundantly than we can either ask or think. Sometimes the
sorrows and difficulties of life may obscure that for us, but it is
there. Just think of the thousands of sermons that are preached
every week to say this—Christ is able to do for us all that we can
require. Just think of the thousands of prayers that are prayed every
week beseeching him to keep his promises and grant to his people
all that they ask of him. After all, what's the good of having Jesus
on the throne if it doesn't mean that unbelievable resources are now
at our disposal both for this world and the next?

Now I realize that even though I have been caricaturing it
somewhat, there is a great deal of truth in what I have just said. What
Christian preacher could stand in a pulpit and deny the joy, the
peace, and the victory that are available in the Christian gospel, that
our ascended Lord and King stands ready to give us? It would
certainly be a foolish thing to try and I want no one to think that I
am trying to do it tonight. But at the same time, if we are to be
faithful to almost the last words Jesus Christ ever spoke to us, I think
we have to remember that those were words not about what we are
to receive but about what we are to do.

There are two moments in this Ascension story which strike me as extremely familiar because they are so much like us. The first is the one I have already mentioned when the disciples asked if now was the time for the restoration of the kingdom. What they were asking, in other words, was whether things were now going to be the way they wanted them to be, whether they could now settle back to enjoy what they were sure they had been striving for and working for ever since they had first met Jesus. Lord, can I now begin to enjoy the fruits of my discipleship? That's essentially their question and, as I say, it should be a very familiar one because we all ask it.

The second moment is when the cloud had obscured their sight and Jesus was no longer visible. It was then that the angels put the question that, by the way, is written right here in our chancel mosaics. "Men of Galilee, why do you stand looking up into heaven?" In both cases, you see, whether it be our Lord speaking his last words or the angels trying to change the disciples' focus after the event had taken place, in both cases the thrust is the same. It is to discourage us from gazing into heaven, looking there for whatever it is we feel we need for our own spiritual well-being, and to refocus our vision somewhere else. *You will bear witness for me.* And that's the Ascension emphasis which I should like to stress this evening. In one of our former hymnals there was an Ascension Day hymn which mercifully has disappeared. Perhaps some of you may recall it. "Golden harps are sounding, angel voices ring" was the opening line. "Pearly gates are opened, opened for the king." But it was the refrain that contained the bad news. "All his work is ended, joyfully we sing; Jesus hath ascended; glory to our King."

"All his work is ended, glory to our King." That's how the church, that's how most Christians have operated. It's all done and all we have to do is to sit and enjoy it until the kingdom comes. "All his work is ended, glory to our King." But that's not the Ascension gospel. Unless I am not reading it right, here at the very point of his departure Jesus is saying that all his work is just beginning and that for the prosecution of that work, he needs you and me. *You will bear witness for me.* If all his work is ended, the church has exactly 120 members, all living in Jerusalem. But another evangelist tells us that his final word was to go into all the world—and again that must mean that his work is just beginning. The hallmark of discipleship is not enjoying what he has to give while singing, "Glory to our King." The hallmark of discipleship is finding the places near and far where we can share what he has to give, the love and the joy and the peace and the forgiveness which we so eagerly claim for ourselves. Stop looking and go! *You will bear witness for me.*

And I think I should point out two reasons why it is at the time of the Ascension that Jesus said this. First of all, we are not going out like bedraggled troops to tell people about a hopeless cause. I know that many Christians give that impression, especially in these days when the church and the gospel, rightly or wrongly, have been under attack from so many directions. Too many of us go out to apologize for what we believe, as though we represented someone who had been whipped off the stage of history, broken and defeated. Not at all. The One who is commanding us to be his witnesses is the one who shares with God in the ultimate control and destiny of the world. The strife is over and the battle is done. All kinds of mopping up operations are being entrusted to you and me, but we must never forget that they are that and nothing more. "You will bear witness for me" was not said by some dying man uncertain of his place in history; it was said by one who knew that history was now in his hands and would remain there until his kingdom had fully come.

The second reason why this was the time for him to say it was clearly put in another of the Ascension stories. The words are so familiar we almost have taken them for granted, but put the two lines together for a moment. *You will bear witness for me... Be assured, I am with you always, to the end of time.* That's the point. The commission he has given us is a staggering one, to be his witnesses in an indifferent or even hostile world. Think of how much more staggering it must have been to that little handful of people, if indeed they had any awareness of the full implications of what he was saying. It's an assignment that anyone would be crazy to tackle by himself, whether in their world or ours.

But now because he is on the throne of the universe, we do not tackle it by ourselves. Luke says that we will receive power from the Holy Spirit. Matthew says that we can count upon his being with us always. Put it either way you like, the reality is the same. When we go, he is with us. When we accept his commission, the power comes. And I do not hesitate to say that it is in our continuing to go that our awareness of his presence is deepened and strengthened. I do not hesitate to say that it is in our continuing to witness that the power grows and increases. I am sure that one of the reasons why we have so little certainty of his presence, so little awareness of the promised power is the simple fact that we sit looking up into heaven and make our religion. But who needs power for that? Who needs any sense of the presence to achieve that? Anyone can stand looking up into heaven! But when we stop looking and go, then the power is there, then the assurance of his presence even to the end of time is real.

I have often wondered why it is that in the Christian church today Easter is such a tremendous celebration and Ascension one which passes by almost without notice. There are a number of cultural reasons I am sure. I dare say that if the commercial world could find something to market on Ascension Day they would soon have everybody celebrating it. But then I think there is this. Whatever happens at Easter, we can't really celebrate Ascension without realizing *our* involvement. Built into the story is the clear implication that we have to do something about it. If the real ruler of this world is not Nixon or Breshnev, if the real ruler of this world is none of the economic cartels, ITT, or the gnomes in Zurich, if the real ruler of this world is Jesus Christ, if you and I really believe that, then we have to do something about it. We cannot treat it as classified information.

Of course, there can be no question about it. If the real ruler of the world is Jesus Christ, then we have to begin by bringing our own lives under his control and being serious about it. That goes almost without saying, but that's only the beginning. If the real ruler of the world is Jesus Christ, then how about my friends, how about my society, how about my community? *You will bear witness for me* is the absolutely inevitable consequence. How can I possibly see other people, other groups behaving as though someone else were in charge and not say something about it, do something about it? If Jesus Christ is a lucky guess or if Jesus Christ is a nice but forlorn hope, then I do what I can when I can. But if Jesus Christ is what this day says he is, the absolute mark to which everything must finally conform, than I have no choice but to give myself totally to the movement. Maybe it's just as well I don't know there is an Ascension Day—look what it gets me involved in!

Sometimes I wonder whether Jesus knew what he was doing when he left and gave the operation essentially over to us. I think we all must wonder, but that really is cynical and distrusting. He did it, and therefore his words must cut through all of our preoccupations and priorities with all the greater force. We have to go back and tell it like it is. Jesus Christ is King. That's not just a pretty phrase. It means that he is the only way that finally works, the only thing that finally lasts. That's what we have to witness to, because unless we have discovered it, what do we have to say, what do we have to do? The Christian gospel is not looking up to heaven waiting for the next thing to come. The Christian gospel is giving everything to see that earth comes under heaven's control. Stop looking and go. *You will bear witness for me... and be assured, I am always with you, even to the end of time.*

Preached at the North Reformed Church, Newark, New Jersey, May 31, 1973.

34

Ascension Day IV

And in him all things hold together.
Colossians 1:17

Back in 1921, the poet William Butler Yeats wrote some of the most frightening lines I know in English literature. They come from a poem called "The Second Coming."

> Things fall apart; the centre cannot hold;
> Mere anarchy is loosed upon the world ...
> The best lack all conviction, while the worst
> Are full of passionate intensity.

Those lines have been in my mind in recent days. How can we read the paper or watch the TV news and not realize that things are falling apart and that the center is not holding? Almost every day brings more news of the passionate intensity of the worst in our society and, while it may not be true that the best lack all conviction, it is certainly true that they don't seem willing to do very much about their convictions.

And I am sure that what we see in our world many of us have experienced in our own lives. For so many people, life has become such a complicated business that they long for the day when things seemed to be simpler, when there were not nearly so many things to worry about, not nearly so many bases that had to be touched. Now it is all they can do to keep some kind of control at least over the things that matter, well aware of how many things fall out of their hands. By the time they pick up that one, they have dropped two more. Things fall apart ... things fall apart.

And then we pick up Paul's letter to the Colossians, and there in the middle of his discussion of Jesus Christ, there is the startling sentence. *In him all things hold together.* Wait a minute, Paul. We wish you would say something more about that. Do you have to make it such a throwaway line? What do you mean that in Jesus Christ all things hold together? How? Why? We need to know, we really need to know.

But having made that throwaway line, Paul is off on something else. The result is that one of the most important sentences in the gospel just stands there by itself, and if you and I want to know what it means, we have to start thinking about it and that is our assignment this morning. Who is right? The poet who says, "Things fall apart; the centre cannot hold." Or the apostle who believed that in Jesus Christ all things hold together? And just how does it work out?

Well, if we want to understand what Paul is getting at, we have to enlarge many of our ideas about Jesus Christ and give them new dimensions. One of the reasons why Paul's assertion doesn't mean too much to many of us is that we have such small ideas about Jesus Christ. We know about the babe in the manger. Of course, we know he grew up to be the humble man of Nazareth; of course we know that he was crucified on Calvary's cross; of course we have some idea about his being raised from the dead on Easter. But none of those or all of them together would seem to warrant the gigantic statement that Paul makes. *In him all things hold together.*

That's because while Paul certainly believed in the babe of Bethlehem, the teacher of Nazareth, the man of Calvary, the risen Lord of Easter—all of that he saw simply as prelude to who it is that Christ is now. He is the personification of God's purpose for the universe. He is not only what God wants this world to be but what God is working to make it. Jesus Christ is not only a picture of what the world could be; he is the picture of what God has determined it surely shall be. That's why *in him all things hold together.*

You see, what you and I need when we look at all the disorganization and confusion of the world in which we live, what we need is what I might call an objective center of reference. That's the only way we can make any sense of it. And in Jesus Christ we have it; he is the plumb line by which everything that happens can be measured and tested. Too many people in our world, including a lot of Christians, don't have such a measuring line. Or if they have one, it's very weak and inaccurate. They measure events by how they affect their happiness or their bank accounts or the well-being of their society. That's nothing.

Paul is inviting us to measure events in the light that God has given us in Jesus Christ. Whatever conflicts with that light is bound to fail no matter who tries it. And how many of the disturbing and frightening things in our world are just that, the result of the world's following something less than the clear command of Christ. Make money your goal instead of human welfare, and you raise up a whole generation of hungry and homeless to haunt you. Make international power your aim instead of brotherhood, and you find yourself in a web of deceit and distrust, as happened just this past week. Make the acquisition of things your purpose instead of sharing and helping, and you have all the insider scandals we have recently read about that have shaken the financial integrity of our nation.

But, you see, in all of these things it is Jesus Christ who is our interpreter. His will, his purpose, they help us understand what is happening, understand it not as meaningless events in a world that is falling apart, but as the inevitable result of a way of life lived in defiance of him. To say that Christ Is Lord, as we do today, is not just to use pretty religious language; it is to affirm that he is the bedrock reality of the universe. Whatever is in accord with his will and purpose will prosper and flourish; whatever is in defiance of them will fall apart and die. For it is *in him that all things hold together.*

I realize that at any given moment it may not look that way; all too often it looks like the other side is winning, and we get flustered and upset. That's where we need to rely on our Ascension faith, our faith that *Christ is Lord,* no matter what the evidence of the moment. Not only must we have that faith, we must act on it, refusing to become enslaved to the spirit of this world but remaining loyally obedient to our Lord no matter what the cost.

I think that's one of the great reasons for coming to church. We need to have our faith in his lordship renewed and strengthened. The world in which we live can give it a dreadful battering in six days. Gathered here beneath the majestic figure in that central mosaic, we can be reassured that he is in charge, that he is in control, not just of us but of the whole world. Someone once said that a good preacher has one eye on the Bible and the other on the morning paper. Well, I should like to alter that. A good Christian has his eye not only on the morning paper, but also on Jesus Christ, for it is by Jesus Christ that he understands the real meaning of the morning paper.

I have seen him in the watchfires of a hundred circling camps,
They have builded him an altar in the evening dews and damps,
I can read his righteous sentence by dim and flaring lamps,
His day is marching on.

Brothers and sisters, in a world in which things seem to be falling apart, believe this, live this. *In Jesus Christ all things hold together.*

But now I think we can make that still more personal. I want us to think about the ways in which Jesus Christ can pull our lives together and unify them. He does that by giving us a purpose that lasts and holds. Aren't you worried about the number of people who simply drift through life trying to cope with each day as it comes? People say that we are raising a whole generation of young people who have no real purpose in life except to get by, but I don't think it's limited to them. What about those whose only purpose seems to be to make money, no matter how, those whose only purpose is their own pleasure, no matter how they get it. Drink, drugs, anxiety—these are some of the prices we pay for no purpose or a purpose that is false and unworthy.

Jesus said that our purpose in life must make us so devoted to God that we become devoted to our brothers and sisters. Humanly speaking, our purpose is finding and maintaining meaningful relationships. There's meaning and purpose that pull life together and give it significance. By myself I mean nothing; living for myself, trying to make whatever I touch turn to my advantage, why, there's no better way to fall apart. It is when we live with all the doors and windows of our lives open to other people, recognizing that we depend on them even as they depend on us, that we begin to discover what life is really all about. And what are we discovering? We are simply discovering what our Lord Jesus Christ has already told us. We can gain the whole world and lose our own souls, but if we are willing to lose our lives for his sake and the gospels, we shall find them. Once again, it is *in him* that *all things hold together.*

I have taken Paul's statement about the cosmic Christ and applied it to the society in which we live and applied it to the conduct of our own personal lives. There was really no reason to divide the Lord up in this way; in either case it is the same Christ and he gives the same command, whether to our society or to us personally: *Follow me.* And when we begin to follow, whether as a society or as individual people, we shall find life begin to come together with healing and strength. Even our times of sorrow and pain become valleys in which we are freshly aware of the healing of his presence. We are able to take things which tear other people apart and leave them broken by the wayside and through the power of Christ let them help us grow into his likeness. Yes, it is often in our pain and brokenness that we find that *in him all things hold together.*

And what about our world? Can we even begin to imagine what it would be like if it took him seriously, seriously enough to take at least a step or two in obedience to him? Well, perhaps we can gain a little idea when we think about a world that refuses to follow him. Our human history is full of them. We have to be realistic, pragmatic, we say. My word, we have been realistic and pragmatic for thousands of years now! How many more lives must be destroyed, how much more blood must be shed, how many more people must suffer in misery and pain before we realize that this is the way to death, that this is the way to be sure that things will surely fall apart? How long, how long?

But there is an answer to that question and we need to think about it. For the promise of our Christian faith is that even now in ways which we cannot begin to understand God is working his purpose out. Even now he is bending our disordered and distracted world into the control of the cosmic Christ.

> God is working his purpose out
>   As year succeeds to year,
> God is working his purpose out
>   And the time is drawing near:
> Nearer and nearer draws the time,
>   The time that shall surely be,
> When the earth shall be filled with the glory of God
>   As the waters cover the sea.

March we forth in the strength of God
  With the banner of Christ unfurled,
That the light of the glorious gospel of truth
  May shine throughout the world:
Fight we the fight with sorrow and sin
  To set their captives free,
That the earth may be filled with the glory of God
  As the waters cover the sea.[1]

  Is life falling apart? Remember, *in him all things hold together.*

Preached at The First Reformed Church, Rochester, New York, May 28, 1987; and at a joint service of the Midland Park (CRC), Faith (RCA), and Irving Park (CRC) Reformed churches, New Jersey, May 24, 1990. This sermon, when preached in May, 1990, alludes to the imminent beginning of the Gulf War.

1 Erik Routley, Ed., *Rejoice in the Lord* (Grand Rapids, Mich.: Eerdmans, 1985), Hymn #425, vs. 1, 3.

Part VI

Pentecost Day

35

Pentecost Day I

I will not leave you comfortless; I will come again to you.
John 14:18

A writer for the magazine, *Life and Work*, the monthly publication of the Church of Scotland, described on the pages of a recent issue an experience she had recently had with a friend. They had for some time been discussing the various fears which are the peculiar property of childhood, the fear of going alone into a dark room, the fear of the creaking of the staircase, the fear of strange people and all of the other things that plague and haunt the minds of children. And after they had finished comparing notes on their own childhood years, going over all the supposed lurking terrors that had frightened them, chuckling softly over many of them, her friend put down his coffee cup and in a sudden moment of seriousness remarked, "Well, amusing as all those things are now that we look back on them, I know myself that there are three fears from which I shall never be free, and I doubt that there is anyone in all the world who can ever be free from them." "And what are those three fears?" she asked. Looking at her for a moment, he replied quietly, "Fear of failure, fear of loneliness, fear of death."

The article does not state the name of the man who thus confessed the inner make-up of his life, but whoever it may have been, in one telling sentence he laid bare the innermost workings of the heart of every one of us. The longer you spend pondering his brief analysis of the human situation, the more clearly you see how deeply he had penetrated into the source of our trouble and unhappiness. For summed up in those three short phrases is the sickness of our hearts. The fear of failure—that numbing, paralyzing feeling that we may not be able to make good, that we shall lose our security, that the things which we have to do may heap up to such gigantic dimensions that we shall not be able to do them—who of us does not know what it means? Who of us does not know the sickening sensation that comes when we think back over what life might have been and then compare it with what we actually have made of it? Who of us does not know that falling feeling in the pit of the stomach when, realizing the slender hold we have on success now, we look into a shadowy unknown future and wonder whether we can keep it going or not? And the fear of loneliness—well in these days of ever-increasing impersonalism and mass movements, which one of us does not know what it means? Our taverns and places of cheap amusement, crowded to the doors with people who have no real friends and are afraid of themselves, are but one indication of the dreadful toll which this fear is taking among us. Our crowded cities with their teeming multitudes, aimlessly wandering they know not where, happy only so long as they are on the go, desperately hungry for some one to smile and to care—well, are we so unfamiliar with the fear of loneliness, the fear of being lost, of ceasing to matter for anyone? And the fear of death—there is nothing in all the world that the modern heart fears more, fears it because it has so largely lost its faith in anything after it. Much as we have tried to gloss it over, to decorate it and soften it, in these past few years death has walked too closely to our doorsteps to let us forget it, and because we no longer understand it, we are afraid of it. Fear of failure, fear of loneliness, fear of death—was not that man almost describing you and me? Truly there is no heart but hath its fears.

I will not leave you comfortless; I will come again to you. That was the promise that our Lord gave to us, a promise that we love to recall for its beauty and tenderness. But beauty and tenderness are not enough for the fears of the human heart. Above all in days like these when we are living in terms of grim realities, when we simply have not the time to let our lives be taken up with anything that will not satisfy, you and I cannot ask about this promise, Is it beautiful? Is it tender? You and I from the fear ridden depths of our spirits can only cry out in agony, Is it true? Did Christ really mean what he was saying, or is it only a very lovely word from a lovely book? For left comfortless we certainly seem to be. There is very little comfort to be found in most of the things in this world, and failure and loneliness and death seem to be the inevitable companions of the journey of every one of us. Can this man Jesus, however beautiful and wonderful and inspiring his own life may have been, can he really come again in person to comfort, to banish fear with love, to strengthen, and to care? O how often we have said it or thought it. "If Christ were here beside me in this, how different my life could be! How little I would dread failure, how little I would fear loneliness, how little I would shrink from death! But he is there and I am here and my heart has its fears."

I will not leave you comfortless; I will come again to you. From that first Pentecost till now, that promise has been true. For that's what we mean by the Holy Spirit, that's what happened on that first Pentecost when the disciples were gathered in the upper room and the Spirit came down upon them like cloven tongues of fire. It was no freak of religious enthusiasm or outburst of wild excess; it was the beginning of a miracle which has persisted in the life of the church down to this very day. For this Spirit was the spirit of Christ, witnessing in their hearts that he was really their Lord, quietly declaring to their spirits that it was true, giving back to them forever the presence and the power that they had had when he had been with them. That's what the Holy Spirit is; Christ come to dwell in each human heart. *I will not leave you comfortless; I will come again to you.* Well, he has come, come in the Holy Spirit at Pentecost, come that the human heart might never again know its fears.

Now the question that all this ought to raise in our minds and hearts is not what happened at Pentecost, but, rather, has Pentecost happened to me? Has this Spirit descended upon me, has my life been opened to the wonder of this abiding presence? Have I understood and believed the wonderful thing that life can be, my life can be, when it has become permeated with the Holy Spirit of Christ? For all too often in our Christian thinking and in our Christian living, we think and act as though we had been left comfortless, as though Christ were a person of long ago from whom we learned lessons, about whom we formed theories and dogmas. Listen, if Christ is for you and me that and nothing more, we are living on the very fringes of glory. For in real Christian faith, Christ is not a person to be talked about, but a presence to be shared, not a history lesson to be studied, but a power to be lived. And power, real Christian power, will not come from the Christ that you and I know about, but from the Christ that you and I have within us. That's what the Holy Spirit means, what Pentecost is here to remind us of—that living, acting, working in our hearts is that same loving power that was working in the person of Jesus of Nazareth nineteen hundred years ago. *I will not leave you comfortless; I will come again to you.*

The Christian faith has ground to a stop in life today just because this source of its power has been forgotten. You and I have so often imagined that the power lay in our ability to study, to reconstruct, to imitate, to trace out the main outlines of the pattern of Christ's life and then go out to reproduce it. Ah, the power never lies in us; it always lies in God. We do not have to imitate Christ; for we can have Christ dwelling in our hearts as this Spirit is shed abroad in them. We do not have to look wistfully back to those days in Galilee and wish we had been there then to see him; for we can see him and know him in the days of our lives as his Spirit descends upon our lives. We do not have to feel comfortless, helpless orphans left alone to battle it out, feverishly trying to understand what he would have us do if he were here; Christ is here at the control of your life and mine, if his Spirit has a strong hold upon our spirits. Once he came, to be sure, and the mystery of that coming still leaves us in awe and wonder. But did you know that he has come again and again and again since then as humble, loyal hearts have been made the dwelling places of his Spirit and so discover that it is really true, that in fact he does walk with us, talk with us, strengthen us, comfort us? *I will not leave you comfortless; I will come again to you.*

There is no heart but hath its fears. Yes, but ponder what the coming of the Holy Spirit means, how it makes of our Christian faith not just a memory of things past, but a living experience of life with Christ, and then go back and look at those same fears. Failure? *I will not leave you comfortless; I will come again to you.* With the disciples on that first Pentecost was Peter, the man who had failed again and again, failed at the most crucial moments, denied and deserted at the crises. Well might he have wondered how with such a record and with such a character he could ever succeed, now that the one influence that could steady him had gone. Then came the Holy Spirit into his life at Pentecost, and Peter became a new man, the mighty rock of the Christian mission and gospel. How? Not simply by trying again and harder—you and I know how far that gets us and how long it lasts! No, there at Pentecost in the Holy Spirit, Peter found one to whom he might take his failures and be forgiven, one who without discouragement would work upon his heart, refining its weaknesses, cleansing its faults, silently but persistently doing it again and again. Yes, Peter found one who even had the power to redeem his failures by turning them into great moments in his life, for he found one who had been able to turn a cross into a symbol of victory. And for Peter, failure held no fear, for his life was now under the control of one who never failed, and that triumphant Spirit was never going to leave him now; it would be the constant companion of his life, turning Peter's failures into God's victories. It's no different today. Christ's own need not fear failure. That's what Pentecost is for! For we do not have to live our lives alone; we can live them in the power of the unfailing Spirit of Christ, the Holy Spirit of Pentecost, who still makes weak hearts strong and feeble wills firm, who still has the power to make a victory out of your failures and mine, if his be the controlling influence in our lives.

Loneliness? *I will not leave you comfortless; I will come again to you.* Somewhere in that upper room on that first Pentecost was Mary the mother of our Lord, and a more lonely woman would be hard to imagine. How would you have felt? Her first-born son had been hanged high on a tree between earth and heaven. She had watched him die; watched her baby until he was a broken and mangled thing on a cross. Truly the sword that pierced his side must have pierced her mother's heart also. And when he had come back alive, scarcely had she had time to recover from her joy, when he was gone again, gone forever into heaven, and she was alone with her memories. Then came the Holy Spirit into her life at Pentecost, and Mary was no longer alone. Jesus was with her. She knew the thrill of his presence again; that wondrous excitement stole over her heart as it did of old when she heard him speak. He had come back—not in the way she expected, but in a way more wonderful, in a way that makes it impossible ever again to lose him. No longer will she sit in her cottage in the purple twilight counting the beads of memory, but now in the golden dawn she recalls, "Lo, I am with you always." How can she be alone? By his Spirit he dwells in her heart. It's no different today. Christ's own never need fear loneliness, for we are not alone. He is with us always as his Spirit steals into our hearts bringing peace, as his word falls upon our ears bringing comfort, as his bread and wine nourish our spirits bringing life.

Death? *I will not leave you comfortless; I will come again to you.* Somewhere in that room on Pentecost was a young man named Stephen, whose life, in a few short weeks, was to be pelted out by the stones of his enemies. He did not want to die; no young man with a future full of promise wants to die. But Scripture says he was a man full of the Holy Spirit for Pentecost had happened, and death now no longer seemed the same. And when the day came and he was dragged outside the city and the stones came crashing against his quivering body, looking up into heaven, he cried, "Lord Jesus receive my spirit." How did that happen? How could one so young, with so much to live for, leave it all with such a cry of assurance and confidence on his lips? Ah, there had come to dwell with him the Spirit of one who had himself faced death with the same confidence, and that Spirit was with Stephen even in that last awful moment, lifting up his dimmed eyes to see the King. It's no different today. Christ's own never need fear death, for he knows death, as only they can know it who have faced it. And his Spirit of triumphant life can grasp our spirits with an iron grip and carry them safely through, if that Holy Spirit, the giver of life, be the source and strength of our life.

Failure? Loneliness? Death? So many Christians think that they ought to pray to be delivered from these things. Christ was not delivered from them. So many Christians think they must work their way through them as best they can. What needless pain. *I will not leave you comfortless.* Every heart has its fears—but the Spirit of God is the answer to those fears, for it is our Christ carrying us through those fears. During the war a young flight lieutenant, about to embark on a dangerous mission, said to his chaplain, "Padre, say a prayer that I get back safely." "No, my son," said the chaplain, "I cannot say such a prayer—not even for myself. But there is one thing I can do, I can come with you." "Christ, save me from failure, from loneliness, from death." No, my child, I cannot do that; I could not even do it for myself. But there is one thing I can do, I can come with you.

I will not leave you comfortless, I will come again to you, and your heart shall rejoice, and your joy no one can take from you.

Preached at the North Reformed Church, Newark, New Jersey, May 25, 1947.

36

Pentecost Day II

*The Spirit itself beareth witness with our spirit,
that we are the children of God.*
        Romans 8:16

... And would you not agree that that is exactly what we need to hear? In fact, this Pentecost finds us once again in that strange, even contradictory, situation that is the peculiar dilemma of modern Christians. On the one hand there is the obvious, the crying need of men and women like you and me for reassurance, for reassurance that runs deep down into life. On the other hand there is the equally obvious fact that the Holy Spirit who, according to the New Testament, is the source of that reassurance, is for most of us less well known and less explored than a planet in outer space. To take the most obvious piece of evidence: We all know what Christmas is all about and we celebrate it widely; Easter is a day that we have no difficulty in understanding or keeping. Even though few of us keep it, we should not experience any trouble in saying what happened on Ascension Day. But what happened on Pentecost? Why should we observe Pentecost? Am I wrong in saying that the day means as little as it does because, frankly, the Holy Spirit means that little in the religion of most of us?

Indeed, if you were to stop to analyze it (and I invite you to do so now) you would have to agree, I think, that the center of the Christian religion as you and I conceive it is the life and teaching of Jesus Christ. To us it seems almost axiomatic that we should come first to Sunday school and then to church to remind ourselves what Jesus did and what Jesus said and then to seek to apply it to our own varied situations. With some of us, in fact, it takes the extreme form of saying that Christianity is the Sermon on the Mount, the Golden Rule, or the general scope of Jesus Christ's sayings. Whoever can master these and put them into practice, in our book that person is a real Christian.

Now I want to point out as strongly as I can that any of the authors of the New Testament would have been completely puzzled by that attitude. True, the four gospels do contain the Sermon on the Mount, the Golden Rule, and the teaching of Jesus, though I should say in passing that they contain a great deal more beside! But you do not have to read the rest of the New Testament from Acts to Revelation very seriously before discovering that the teachings of Jesus interest these people surprisingly little. The center of their faith, the living, throbbing thing that runs all through it, is the presence of the Holy Spirit. No questions about it; the Christian gospel for them was not a body of teaching, but the living experience of a living presence which touched and transformed every day that they lived. Every time they looked around, they felt the Spirit.

Like us, they had the life, the death, the teaching, the example of their Lord to look back to. And yes, like us, though surely more fervently, they had the promise that he would come again in glory to look forward to. But now pause there for a moment and ask yourself what exactly between that past and that future you and I have to talk about in the present? Not much, is there? Then ask yourself about the present tense of their religion, and from almost every page the answer comes ringing with excited triumph, the

Spirit of God, that Spirit that *beareth witness with our spirit that we are the children of God.*

You see, the exciting thing about the Christianity of the New Testament was almost the very thing that has disappeared from the Christianity of the twentieth century. There is hardly a religion in the world that does not have sacred teachings from the past, whether they be good, bad, or indifferent. There is hardly a religion in the world that does not have some shape of the future drawn in golden strokes. But there is no religion in all the world except the Christian faith that says that God dwells in ordinary human lives, touching, transforming, glorifying them each and every day, in every kind of situation. There is no religion in all the world except the Christian faith that offers us not just a book about the past or some visions of the future, but a living presence. Perhaps on this Pentecost morning we need to have another look at the religion we profess and so sadly misunderstand.

The Spirit itself beareth witness with our spirit that we are the children of God. That was Saint Paul's glowing account of it, and you may be sure that he was speaking hot from the heart out of his own pulsating experience. There had been times when he had wondered frankly whether human beings were anything more than children of chance, times when he had been tempted to forsake the imperious claims of love and follow the dark passions and low aims of the baser self. But every time he had found himself listening to those cynical promptings within his own mind and heart, a powerful voice was heard reminding him, "No, no; you are a child of God."

Or there had been times when in bitter disappointment and great sorrow, problems besetting Saint Paul on every side, none of which would he have encountered if he had stuck with his tentmaking and let Christ alone, times when he could not help asking how there could be a God, how there could be a Father, how he could be love and let this happen; times when he had to ask whether they were not right who looked up into the heavens above and saw nothing. But every time he felt forsaken, alone, lost, there was that still, small voice within that kept repeating, "Even in the lostness of the moment, even in the forsakenness, you are not alone; you are a child of God."

I do not think I should be wrong in saying that there were times in Saint Paul's life, for he was a proud man, when he felt himself on top of the world, when he knew the thrill of power within his grasp, success within his reach. Everything was going as he had wanted it, all of the disordered pieces were falling into place. At last he could take pride in his achievements, glory in his success. But every time he felt that surge of self-confidence, that comfortable warmth of self-esteem, there was the discomfort of that disquieting word that would not be silenced, "Will you let your own success make you forget that you are not your own master? You are the child of God."

Now I suspect that even as I have been reciting what must have been the apostle's experience, all of you have been saying to yourselves, "Well, I have known something like that." Bless your hearts, of course you have. The Spirit of God has not been dead these nineteen hundred years. All of us have known those strange and sudden moments of awareness and resistance in temptation, of courage and strength in sorrow, of humility and dedication in prosperity and success. What we may not have realized is that it is exactly those moments, for which sometimes we find it hard to account, that the New Testament means it when it speaks about the Holy Spirit. It was no fairy godmother that brought you to yourself in time to resist that temptation. It was no mere chance that picked you up and set you on your feet in your time of need. It was no lucky star that you have to thank for keeping your head in prosperity. It was Pentecost; it was the Spirit of God reminding you that you are the child of God, making real to you at the moment of your need the possibilities which you have. Every time you were able in any situation to be what you ought to have been, every time you felt the Spirit. *The Spirit itself beareth witness with our spirit that we are the children of God.*

We have all had these moments. But, let's confess it, that's pretty much what they are in the lives of most of us—moments, occasions when the Spirit of God has been able to break through our clay-shuttered doors. But how quickly they swing to again. Moments...did you ever stop to think of this? Take those moments, those really great moments in life when you have risen to the occasion, met the challenge, when you have resisted temptation, when you have stood up to suffering with a smile, when you have kept your balance in success, when you have lived like God's child...moments. Why can't all life be like that? Why can't every day be like that day when you did it? Why must there be these long stretches of drab and dirty living between the moments on the mountain? Why can't every day be touched with the same glory, informed with the same victory?

Well, the clear message of the gospel is that it can be. Jesus Christ came to this earth and died and rose again to make us the children of God. But that's so far back in the past we easily lose sight of it in the rush and press of living. God has great purposes for a kingdom in which someday all shall live as his children. But that's so far in the distant future that the sights and scenes of the present obscure it. But here is the Spirit of God speaking to your spirit, wherever you are, speaking in the rush and press, speaking across the sights and scenes, saying, not in some past event, not in some future hope, but, because of Jesus Christ, in present reality, "You are the child of God," and saying it not just at moments; saying it every day, saying it in every event of our lives. To hear it, we have only to break open those self-imposed prison bars and let the winds of God blow in. *The Spirit itself beareth witness with our spirit that we are the children of God.*

To speak historically, that's what happened that first Pentecost when 120 Christians (there were no more in all the world) were waiting in that upper room. In a burning moment of discovery, they found God not in the past, not in the future, but in the present, saying the thing that they needed to hear, just at the moment they needed to hear it. They could and they did face anything after that because they were convinced that they were not alone. Never were they without the reminder that, no matter how bleak or unpromising the moment, they had everything that God could give, even his presence with them. Pentecost was the beginning of a triumphant experience that nothing could break because it was the beginning of their certainty that the Spirit of God dwelt within them.

But to speak historically and stop there is almost to blaspheme. For what was so different about them from us? Nothing. The same possibility, the same power, the same Pentecost is waiting for you and me to claim it. How many people there are walking through life with a bag of theological bones that they think is the gospel! How many people there are walking through life with an armful of textbooks on morality that they think are the Christian religion! How many of us there are sitting in church this Pentecost morning whose religion is entirely tied to a dead past or a rather indefinite future. Well, here in all the fullness of its power is a faith written entirely in the present tense. Jesus Christ did not cease to act when he ascended into heaven. God is not sitting on his hands, waiting for things to get so bad that he can wind up the story of the world. The Spirit of Jesus Christ, the Spirit of the living God is standing by the door of the life of every last one of us, waiting, wanting to come in to start things happening with us now!

One day in the year 1830 in the little Scottish town of Port Glasgow, James Macdonald came home at suppertime with his brother George. As was their custom every evening, they went into the room of their invalid sister. But this night as they watched her, they were sure that the end was near. She lay on her couch, fevered, and murmuring incoherently. But gradually they became aware that she was praying, praying for the presence of the Holy Spirit. James stood by the window for a moment and then quietly said, "I have got it." Walking to his sister's bed he took her hand and said, "Arise and stand upright." At once she got up, walked with them to the supper table completely cured. The next day she wrote of her experience to an invalid friend, Mary Campbell, who lived across the Clyde. And Mary Campbell folded the letter, and got up herself, healed and restored.

It's a parable of what happens every time you feel the Spirit. New people from old, with new attitudes, new outlooks, new relationships, new possibilities, new goals, new directions, new minds, new hearts, yes, even new bodies. For that same Spirit that reminds us that we are the children of God makes us the children of God. Every time I feel the Spirit, I know that God is my Father, I know that Christ is my Savior, I know that nothing can separate me from that love. Every time I feel the Spirit I know that nothing can prevent me from living as a child of God.

The Spirit itself beareth witness with our spirits that we are the children of God.

Preached at the North Reformed Church, Newark, New Jersey, May 17, 1959.

37

Pentecost Day III

Thou sendest forth thy spirit, they are created:
and thou renewest the face of the earth.
    Psalm 104:30

Let's begin at the beginning this Pentecost morning. "In the beginning God created the heaven and the earth." And what, you may ask, has that to do with Pentecost, the Feast of the Holy Spirit? In fact, it almost seems a confusing way to begin a sermon on the Holy Spirit. For the Holy Spirit, heaven knows, is an obscure enough idea about which we contemporary Protestants know little or nothing. We use the name frequently enough, at least in our hymns and forms of public worship, but we really could not give much of an account if we were called upon to do so. It wouldn't hurt us to hear a sermon on the Holy Spirit or even to do some homework about the Spirit. But if that's what you intend doing this morning, domine, why start off with the creation of the world, which strikes us as a pretty remote place from which to begin? After all, "Creator of heaven and earth" comes pretty early along in that creed that we said a little while ago, while "the Holy Ghost" comes pretty near the end of it. Why not begin where our problem is? Who or what is this Holy Spirit?

227

I rather imagine, though you may not at first see it, that I have begun where our problem is. "In the beginning God created the heaven and the earth." What picture comes to your mind as you hear those words? Millions, billions, trillions of years ago, as science would tell us, there was some kind of great cosmic upheaval after which out of nothing there emerged the stars in their courses, an infinite number of universes all stretching out endlessly in space. God created—something which happened way back there; and then it was done and the story moves on to other points of interest. That's about the way we think of it, isn't it? Even there, however, while the first verse in the Bible says, "In the beginning God created the heaven and the earth," I would remind you that the second verse says, "The Spirit of God moved upon the face of the waters." But that's a clue to which we may return a little later.

What I am trying to say now is simply this. In our common patterns of believing, the way we think of creation makes us think of God as a very remote person both in time and in space. Infinite years ago, God did it. Ever since then the world has been running along. Save for an occasional minor catastrophe or the unusual freak like a comet, the universe runs itself while, from some incredibly distant point in space, God looks down and superintends the operation. We can pray to God; we can ask for help and guidance; we certainly should seek his providence and protection. But it's a self-contained world, isn't it, created and given to us long, long ago. And God sits somewhere outside of it. Have I been fair to the way in which most of us think about this matter, if indeed we think at all?

Well, that's not the way the Bible thinks, especially the New Testament. This is the point I want to make. While certainly the New Testament never doubts that in the beginning God created the heaven and the earth, it also remembers that that was only the beginning. Ever since then, God has been working on it, from the inside, not from the outside, remaking it, reshaping it, recreating it. And the end is not yet nor will it come until the world which was created has been recreated to be a perfect reflection in all its parts of Jesus Christ. This, as Saint Paul reminds us, was the purpose God had from the beginning, a purpose that you and I who know Jesus Christ know and understand, a purpose to which God will adhere until it has been accomplished. Yes, if you like, the material stuff of the world was created way back there. But that's the least of it. The more important stuff of the world is still being created and will continue to be until the creator's purpose has been fulfilled.

Now if all that strikes you as a pretty heady business, let me say that it is. I think we need to remind ourselves that the Christian gospel is more than something for you in your small corner and me in mine. Especially in this space age, we need to remind ourselves that the Christian gospel has cosmic dimensions, has always had them. But though these may not be easy to grasp, I think I have said two things which are not difficult to understand, even though they may represent a small revolution in our usual way of thinking. God is still creating; God has not finished with his plan. And he is at work from the inside. There are no more cosmic upheavals as there may have been trillions of years ago. Silently, almost imperceptibly, God creates his changes and his transformations from within.

And that's what we mean by the Holy Spirit. I don't know why it should give us such trouble. The Holy Spirit is simply the church's way of saying that our God is not absent from human life, but is here in it, not as an absentee landlord who surveys his possessions from a comfortable and safe distance. God is totally and completely involved with the creation he has made, nearer than hands and feet and closer than breathing. Bishop Robinson in his much discussed book, *Honest to God*, makes a great deal out of the fact that many people are distressed by a Christianity which teaches that God is "out there." Well, the Christianity which they know is badly incomplete. For the enormous emphasis of the New Testament upon the Holy Spirit is simply saying that God is also "in here"— in the social processes of history, in the thinking and planning of our minds, in the whole pattern of human existence and human relationships. "Whither shall I go from thy presence or whither shall I flee from thy Spirit?" asks the psalmist. It can't be done. For the Spirit is God interpenetrating every aspect of his creation.

Now while this has many many implications, there is one about which I want to speak this morning. This Spirit who is present in the whole pattern of being is present as the creator. As at the beginning, wherever the Spirit of God is, things are being made, shaped, renewed. *Thou sendest forth thy Spirit, they are created: thou renewest the face of the earth.* To have the Spirit in our midst is not simply to have a nice comforting presence. Yes, it is to have that all right. Who can believe that God is in the midst of us and not be comforted? But to have the Spirit in our midst is to have things happening to us. And these things can be very disturbing, as we are changed from old patterns into new ones, stirred out of sleepy ways into vital ones, forced out of comfortable olds ruts into strange new adventures. The Spirit is never static, but always dynamic. Wherever the Spirit comes, the Spirit makes changes, transforms, creates, and renews. *Thou sendest forth thy Spirit, they are created: thou renewest the face of the earth.*

I think that this is important because, frankly, many of us do not expect it or even want it. In some way or another in this affluent America of ours, we have the idea (though we are by no means the first people in history to have it) that religion is something that should never change. Indeed, as many of us see it, its function is to preserve and even to sanctify with its blessing the patterns which we have, patterns which are being threatened on so many sides. In church, of all places, we should feel that the old ways are still the good ways, the safe and sound ways. In church we do not want to be disturbed but rather confirmed and strengthened in what we have already come to believe.

And we are a little upset and want perhaps to blame the minister when just the reverse begins to happen; when religion and church, so far from sanctifying our accepted patterns, make us question them; when we find our faith forcing us to new ideas, confronting us with new people, making us uncomfortable unless we rethink whole questions which we had long ago assumed were settled. What is still worse, we feel threatened by this kind of religion because it often puts its most significant questions exactly to those ways of doing things to which we have been most deeply committed—our patriotism, our economy, our social practices, even our long cherished personal opinions.

If you have had an experience like this and want to blame anybody, I suggest that you blame the Spirit of God, that creator spirit, who renews the face of the earth. For the blunt truth is, my friend, that God has not finished with you and me any more than God has finished with his Church, any more than God has finished with his world. God is still making them, and the making can sometimes be a painful business as creativity often is. This is after all what happens when we are foolish enough to let God into our lives. We have a nice little niche for God with a couple of candles burning and flowers there in season. We say, "Welcome, it is so good to have you," because we know how many times God can be helpful to us. But then we begin to discover that this God is like one of those irritating boarders who will not stay in his room. God begins to criticize the way the house is run, offers rather caustic comments about the occupant of the home. First thing we know, without asking anybody's by-your-leave, God starts redecorating, or even putting in new wiring. Then one night we come home to find the boarder standing in the front door and saying, "Come on, we're moving out of here entirely; this house isn't adequate for your needs."

Well, now, something very much like that is what happens when the Spirit of God, the creator spirit, invades our lives. God cannot, will not, let them alone. For while we may be rather proud of our lives and somewhat defensive about them, God knows (and I think we do too) what shabby things they really are. The personalities of most of us are like houses in which we have lived for many years. We have lived there so long and are so attached to them that we really don't notice that the paint is peeling, the plaster cracked, that the kitchen stove doesn't work properly, the furniture is worn and shabby. Or if we do see it, we say, "Well, it's mine and I like it."

But once the Spirit of God, the creator spirit, gets hold of those personalities, that's all over with. The little hatreds and jealousies, the narrowness and bitterness with which, like the peeling paint and cracked plaster, we have lived so long we are fond of them, they have to go. For where the Spirit of God is, there is creation, there is renewal. God is not content with what exists. God knows the master plan; knows how far short of it you and I are. Friend, when the Spirit comes into your life, there will be changes. *Thou sendest forth thy Spirit, they are created: thou renewest the face of the earth.*

The same thing is true of the church. After all, the church, as Saint Paul somewhere calls it, is the fellowship of the Spirit. I could almost say that it is the instrument through which the creative work of the Spirit goes on in this world. And can we suppose that that church will be allowed to become petrified in its own way, dedicated to the preservation of what it is and has? Some of you may know that for the past year or so I have been working on a history of the Christian Church for young people. It has now gone to the publisher and will be out sometime next fall. Well, time and again as I was reading and studying for that book, I was impressed by the same fact. Over and over again in history, the church became so rigid, so defensive, so insensitive to the world around it that any good historian would know that nothing could save it. But always at those moments in its history, the church experienced renewal, reformation. We speak about the Reformation and we should, more often than we do. But actually there have been many reformations in the history of the church. And, don't you see, there will be, there must be many more. We may be living through one right now and not quite realizing it. For how can we say as a church that with all our laziness, indifference, and ineptness, we are perfect servants? Sometimes the machinery will creak and the gears will grind. Sometimes it will mean giving up things we thought we could not do without. But the creator spirit is always at work moving

God's people out of the church that was, into the church that shall be. And where the Spirit is not present in creative power, the church is dead.

And the world? Yes even in the world of 1964, sophisticated, scientific, technological, *thou sendest forth thy Spirit, they are created: thou renewest the face of the earth*. Once again we are distressed by the ferment of the nations, by the strident and often angry cries of groups who want their due or perhaps a little more than their due. And we are annoyed and disturbed because the old order of things as we have known it seems likely to be swept away as in a flood. Well, I am not now seeking to justify any and every political and social movement which rises in these troubled days. But I am saying that if you suppose that the Spirit, the creator spirit, is content with western civilization as it is, you do not know the Spirit's dynamic. Justice and righteousness for all people are the goals of creation, and God will not rest until they have been accomplished, nor will God hesitate to use all the forces of history for the achievement of that purpose.

"Come, Creator Spirit" was one of the ancient prayers of the church. Knowing its implications, do we dare to pray it this Pentecost morning? We must. For while its answer will always mean disturbance and change, it will also mean life and joy and peace as we share in the coming of God's Kingdom. *Thou sendest forth thy Spirit, they are created: thou renewest the face of the earth.*

Come, Creator Spirit.

Preached at the North Reformed Church, Newark, New Jersey, May 17, 1964.

38

Pentecost Day IV

*The day shall come when I will pour out my Spirit on all
mankind: your sons and your daughters shall prophesy,
your old men shall dream dreams and your young men
see visions: I will pour out my Spirit in those days even
upon slaves and slave girls.*
  Joel 2:28-29

The day shall come... Well, if the New Testament is to be
believed, the day has come. Our problem would seem to be that it
may have gone right past us without our realizing it. Joel lived in a
time in which religion was the monopoly of a carefully selected
group of people. There were priests and there were ecclesiastical
lawyers who alone had the right and the authority to speak for God,
while it was up to everyone else to listen and obey. Once in a great
while, as in the case of Amos the sheep farmer from Tekoa,
someone broke out of this box and claimed to be speaking for God,
even though he did not belong to the properly appointed class. But
the reception that was given to Amos by the religious establishment
was a pretty good indication of the general feeling about such
unauthorized activity. Sheep farmers should tend their sheep and
mind their own business. They were meant to listen to their
religious betters, who alone had the right and the authority to be
spokesmen for the Lord.

That was the background against which Joel spoke. We do not know all that much about him; indeed we cannot be certain whether he himself belonged to the official religious establishment or not. Some scholars think that he may have held a minor office in the Jerusalem priesthood, while others maintain that he was more vaguely associated with the temple as one of the recognized group of prophets. There is even a wide variety of opinion as to when in Hebrew history he wrote this little book. It really doesn't make any difference who he was or when he wrote. The point is that he was obviously chafing under the system, that he looked for and longed for the coming of that time when the arrangement would be different, that time when there would be no class of religious experts because all of God's people would possess his Spirit from the oldest to the youngest, from the most important to the lowest. *The day shall come when I will pour out my Spirit on all mankind: your sons and your daughters shall prophesy, your old men shall dream dreams and your young men shall see visions: I will pour out my Spirit in those days even upon slaves and slave girls.*

Now the New Testament claims that that has happened, happened on the occasion that we celebrate today, happened on the Day of Pentecost when the little company of Christians was gathered waiting in the Upper Room. The Spirit came upon them and all sorts of things began to occur. Lest there be any misunderstanding as to the meaning of these events, Peter stood up and said, "This is what the prophet spoke of," and then went on to cite the very words of Joel that I have quoted. The day to which he had looked forward so anxiously and so eagerly had now come. There were no more religious experts; from now on, all of God's children could dream and speak and act for him.

Although I have no desire to engage in a history lesson this Pentecost morning, I do have to point out the strange way in which the church has refused to take either Joel or Peter seriously. We all know how in the course of Christian history there developed the

same rigid kind of religious establishment that Joel had known in
Jerusalem. Pope and bishop and priest—they were, if not the Lord's
anointed at least appointed. They represented God officially; they
spoke for God, while the rest of the people were expected again to
listen and obey. That very pattern which Peter said had disappeared
on Pentecost gradually re-emerged and became the standard for the
Christian world.

You and I like to think that it was the Reformation that broke that
pattern up and went back to the vision of Joel and Peter. In a way
I suppose it did—or at least it tried to; certainly we have no such
rigid establishment as before. But even a quick look at our situation
should be enough to convince us that we still have an establishment.
Ministers and preachers may not be people whom we feel we must
hear and obey, but by and large we are content to let them do the
thinking about God and the speaking for God, to let them do the
dreaming and see the visions while the rest of us go about our
business as usual. Protestants have been able to bypass Pentecost
just as successfully as the people of the Middle Ages or the Jews in
Jerusalem. "The day shall come," says Joel. "The day has come,"
says Peter, but not so far as most Christians of the twentieth century
are concerned. We should be just as shocked to see an automobile
mechanic or a short-order cook stand up in our midst and say,
"Thus says the Lord," as the men of Israel were when that sheep
farmer Amos appeared in the midst of their festival. Where did *he*
go to school? Who ordained him? Let's have a look at his credentials!

It is a frightening thing, this claim that all of God's children can
speak for him, and I suppose that some of the excesses of the
Pentecostal movement in our own time make us all the more
frightened. It could and does sometimes lead to such wild disorder.
But before we let that prospect scare us off completely, let's try to
understand what it is that both Joel and Peter are wanting to say to
us when they tell us that the day has come when I pour out my Spirit
on all mankind.

First and most basically, Pentecost says that to be close enough to God to share fully in his presence and power is open to everyone, whether we be bishop or dishwasher, whether we be abbess or housewife. Living with God now belongs to all of us. The fact that you and I really have not seen that comes out in a number of ways. For example, we talk about the saints as though they were a select group of holy people, the great heroes of the faith who belong in stained-glass windows. But in the New Testament the saints are the members of any congregation. All Christ's people are saints, because all of them can live close enough with God to share fully in his power and presence.

Or again, we have a way of saying, "Even though I am a member of the church, I'm not really a very religious person." I'm never very sure what people mean when they say that, but if they mean that God is not as close and real to them as he is to the minister, they have missed the Christian point completely and in missing it have missed so much that could fill their lives with meaning and joy. This is why Christ came; he said it over and over again and in many different ways. He came so that the gap between you and me and God could be completely closed, so that you and I could look up and say Father and mean it with all the content that Jesus said it and meant it. I think of the old spiritual, "You got wings, I got wings, all God's children got wings." Well sure enough, they do—we do. We all have wings to carry us in any situation out of our despair, out of our difficulty, straight to the loving and powerful presence of God. *I will pour out my Spirit on all mankind*—and God has, God has. Get him off his high and distant throne into the midst of life with all of its baffling problems. That's where Jesus Christ declared he wants to be and will be. The presence and the power of God know no limits, no class, no official status. They are yours and they are mine in the presence of the Spirit God has given us, whoever we are, wherever we are. *I will pour out my Spirit on all mankind.*

But that glorious fact can have a little sharper definition, I think. *Your sons and your daughters shall prophesy*. That word, I know, has all kinds of unhappy connotations. It suggests to us reading palms, gazing into crystal balls, looking at tea leaves—the sort of business that increasingly we seem to see opening up on the streets of Newark. And since fortune-telling is not something most of us want to do, we can do without Joel's word about our being able to prophesy.

But that is to prostitute the word "prophecy". That word really adds another dimension to our sharing with God. Not only do we share his power and his presence, we also share his purpose. Too often the way we Christians share God's presence is shapeless and selfish. We simply use it for our own comfort and advantage. It's the added dimension of purpose that gets us up and moving, sometimes uncomfortably.

I know that when many folks hear about following the purpose of God in their lives, they immediately have all kinds of questions to raise. How can I possibly know what that purpose is in all of the complications of human existence in this time? What really is right and what is wrong? Well, I know that there are problems, but I don't think it is all that difficult if we keep one thing clearly in mind. The purpose of God has been defined as sharply and as clearly as possible in Jesus Christ. How to translate him into the decisions and reactions of our lives may not always be easy, but we know the purpose because we know Jesus.

Now the power to see that and the power to do something about it are ours in the Spirit. For the life of me I don't know why people should think that speaking in tongues or dancing in the aisle are a greater indication of the presence of the Spirit than lives of love and service. What did Paul say to his friends in Corinth? After he had paid his respects to all their ecstatic things, remember that he went on to say he would now show them the best way of all. "I may speak in tongues of men or of angels, but if I am without love, I am a sounding gong or a clanging cymbal" (1 Cor. 13:1).

You can't put it more clearly than that, can you? If prophesying means speaking for God, then what speaks more clearly than a life lived out in commitment to love? But that kind of life anyone of us can live. We don't need to be set apart or ordained to do it; it's not limited to the so-called religious. *Your sons and your daughters shall prophesy. Even slaves and slave girls shall have my Spirit.* The loving purpose of our God made real and clear in Jesus Christ can be re-enacted in the life of each and every one of us—must be re-enacted in the life of each and every one of us—or the church becomes limp and lame and the cause of the kingdom struggles and suffers. God's presence, God's power, God's purpose—you and I can have them all in the daily business of our lives. *I will pour out my Spirit on all mankind: your sons and your daughters shall prophesy.*

But one thing more, and for me who am in the middle years of life, this is perhaps the most significant of all. I don't suppose that we see anything unusual in Joel's prediction that the young will see visions. The idealism of the young is something we all know about, whether we like it or not. Sometimes we admire it, while at other times we wish that young people would pay a little more attention to reality and less to their starry-eyed ideals.

But, *Your old men shall dream dreams*.... There is the strange one. In our culture, especially in our culture, we settle down so quickly and so easily to things as they are, to hard-nosed reality as we like to call it. Listening to the young, we shake our heads wisely and say, "Just wait till they grow up a little—they'll learn. We'll see what happens to their fancy ideas then." And so we sit with our broken dreams and our empty visions, unhappily taking what is as what must be. Do you remember T. S. Elliot's "Hollow Men"?

> This is the dead land... This is cactus land...
> In this valley of dying stars
> In this hollow valley
> This broken jaw of our lost kingdoms.

Well, we know the place, don't we, the cactus land, the valley of dying stars. And perhaps one great reason why we are so defensive about the dreams and visions of the young is that we once had them too, once shared all kinds of high ideals and lofty goals before they turned to nothing, and life began to take us through cactus land and into the valley of dying stars.

Maybe Joel's promise to people like us is only a distant whisper, but how we need to hear it. *Your old men shall dream dreams.* It doesn't have to go. We don't need to live in cactus land or in the valley of dying stars! Because God pours out his Spirit on all of us, regardless of our age, regardless of our experience or worldly wisdom, our faith in the future, God's future, God's future made clear in Jesus Christ, that faith is always being renewed, always being freshened and made stronger. Maybe some of the visions and dreams of our youth needed clarifying and sharpening. But if anything, now they should be stronger because of all we have shared with God and God with us. I remember once hearing my father say that he believed far less than he did as a young man, but that he believed it with far greater conviction and intensity.

That should be true of all of us, I think. That's the work of the Spirit—to deepen and to intensify our trust in the promises. That's how we stay young, by keeping clearly in front of us the vision of what must surely be and never letting it fade because the Spirit of the living God keeps the vision, the dream, fresh, alive and real. *I will pour out my Spirit on all mankind.... Your old men will dream dreams and your young men see visions.* There is no old age in the kingdom of God, in the life of the Spirit. There are only those who are still growing in eager anticipation of what is yet to be because God has promised it in Jesus Christ our Lord.

J. B. Phillips, whose paraphrase of the New Testament I know many of you have enjoyed, once put it this way: "Every time we say 'I believe in the Holy Spirit,' we mean that we believe that there is a living God able and willing to enter human personality and change it." A living God able and willing to enter human personality and change it... *I will pour out my Spirit on all mankind.* That was once the promise; that now is the reality for all of us. And may the God of hope fill you with all joy and peace by your faith in him until by the power of the Holy Spirit you overflow with hope.

Preached at the North Reformed Church, Newark, New Jersey, June 10, 1973.